That's SCOOP
£1·45

Just some of the big names you'll find inside this year's SCOOP ANNUAL...

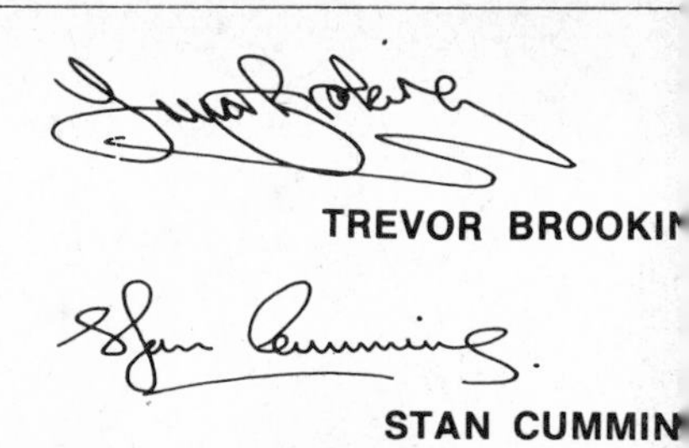

CONTENTS

STORIES

PIN-UPS

STAR FEATURES

SPECIAL FEATURES

To Gordon Xmas 1981 Love Dad & Mum.

RAY WILKINS

IVAN MAUGER

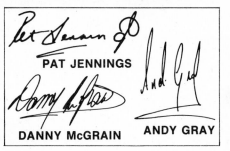

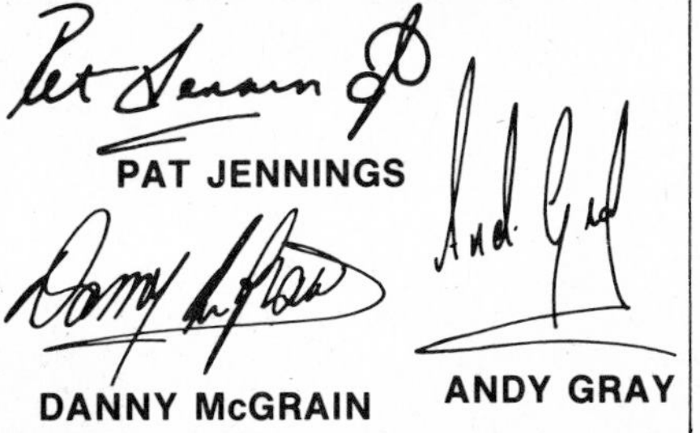

PAT JENNINGS

DANNY McGRAIN

ANDY GRAY

PETER SHILTON

KENNY DALGLISH

GOODYEAR
KENNY
GOODYEAR
CHAMPION
GREGG
BARRY
SUZUKI
CHAMPION

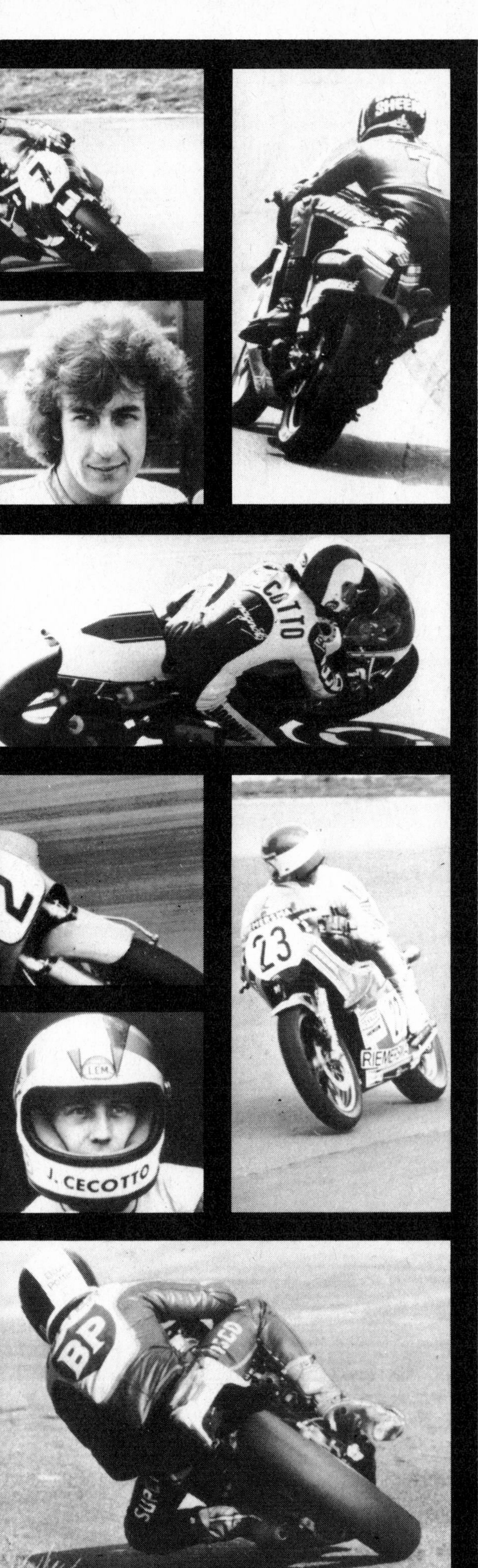

MOTOR-CYCLE RACERS

FOCUS ON SPEED

Motor cycle racing has become respectable — that's the biggest and best boost the sport has been given in the past ten years. The sport has progressed from its oily, black leather image, where non-enthusiasts were hard-pushed to recognise even the top riders, to the point where today's stars attend garden parties at Buckingham Palace !

Barry Sheene, Phil Read and Mike Hailwood have all been awarded the M.B.E. for their services to motor cycle racing — and with good reason. They have been able to project an articulate and colourful image of the sport — as well as providing top-class racing thrills. Read and Hailwood may now have hung up their leathers, but the highly-popular Sheene is more than capable of carrying the flag as Britain's leading ambassador of the sport.

SPORTING HERO

His brightly-coloured leathers, his distinctive racing number 7 and his television appearances have made him instantly identifiable. Added to that, his World Championship successes have given Britain a sporting hero to be proud of.

Not unexpectedly, Barry is also involved in the sport's latest development — the World Series. He and Kenny Roberts, that American ace of pace, led the world's top riders into a championship series intended to improve the lot of the riders both on and off the track.

SPONSORSHIP

Because of the time and money needed to maintain today's sophisticated racing machines, a "privateer" has little chance of success against the professional team riders in the international arena. It's works backing or sponsorship that can turn a good rider into a top star — but ironically, while Barry Sheene and motor cycle racing go hand in hand in this country, there have been few home riders following in his tyretracks.

His occasional team-mate at Suzuki, Steve Parrish, has been Britain's brightest prospect for so long that he's in danger of drifting into motor racing because of lack of sponsorship. Few others have shown the inclination to move into the international scene and while hopes are high for Ron Haslam, Keith Huewen, Alex George and Steve Manship, Britain has fallen behind in the championship stakes.

Venezuelan Johnny Cecotto, Australian Greg Hansford, South African Kork Ballington, Dutchman Wil Hartog, Japanese Katayama Katazumi, Italian Graziano Rossi — these, along with the multi-talented Americans, are the names that have burst into the front ranks of the sport, without a serious British challenger in sight.

BIGGER AND BETTER

However, the British scene is not all gloom and dismay. The club racing calendar is packed with high quality events, and the Isle of Man TT races are, if possible, even more popular than ever, with speeds increasing and lap times round the 37-mile circuit sent crashing annually. Added to that, international meetings at Oulton Park, Donington and Brands Hatch consistently thrill the fans — not forgetting the British Grand Prix at Silverstone, the GP that's tops with the riders as well as the fans.

And because of its ever-increasingly professional attitude, the sport is ready to add to the advances of the past few years. Motor cycle racing isn't just here to stay — it's getting bigger and better!

STARK

MATCHWINNER FOR HIRE
JON STARK
£1000 PER MATCH
PLUS £250 PER GOAL
NO PAYMENT FOR LOST GAME

Too late with your tackle, chum!

GREAT GOAL, STARK!

F.A. official Clive Smith is watching.

With three goals, you've plenty to smile about today, Stark – but you won't be smiling for long! I'm going to put you and your kind out of football – **FOR GOOD!**

Smith works fast. When Stark turns up the following Saturday to play for First Division Stansfield Rovers . . .

Don't bother unpacking your gear, Jon. This ruling has just arrived from the F.A. banning all mercenaries!

I'll bet Clive Smith's behind this. He's been trying to shove the mercenaries out of football ever since he was appointed to the F.A.!

All over Britain, freelance players are being told they're finished. Stark's sidekick, Cosmo Kent, is one of them . . .

It's a downright liberty! We gotta do something about this!
Too right, Cosmo. Come on, we've got some people to see . . .

Two days later, Jimmy Sloane, manager of Fourth Division strugglers Weedilstone Athletic, receives some visitors . . .
I . . . I don't believe it, Stark! You . . . you mercenaries want to play for Weedilstone Athletic . . . for NOTHING!
Too right! The F.A. can't stop us playing if we all sign up for a team under the ordinary rules. And now we'll prove we're the best in the game.

The fools! Stark and his cronies have signed for Weedilstone! When are they going to realise their days of big money football are finished?
WEEDILSTONE SIGN THE SUPERSTARS

Stark sets out to prove Smith wrong. The mercenaries' first game is against league leaders Warnton Town.
We're beginning to get it together. There's space for Cosmo in the middle.

First time Weedilstone have scored in three games!
GOAL!

It's the start of a rout.
That's 3-0 to us!
AND NUMBER FOUR!

Warnton collapse in the second half . . .
Eight nil with only a few seconds to go. I feel sorry for these blokes – but this is all part of my plan.
Enjoy your fun while it lasts, Stark. But how long will you get a kick out of Fourth Division soccer, I wonder?

Weedilstone go from strength to strength.

SPORT WEEDILSTONE WIN 10-NIL
STARK CHALLENGES THE LEAGUE CHAMPS AND F.A. CUP HOLDERS – DECLARES HIS TEAM CAN BEAT ANYTHING IN ENGLISH FOOTBALL...

STARK MUST BE MAD! I'm sure the League and League Cup holders Cherton will be delighted to cut him down to size!
HEAR! HEAR!

It's worked! We play Cherton next Wednesday . . . a sponsored game for one hundred thousand pounds.
Great stuff, man.

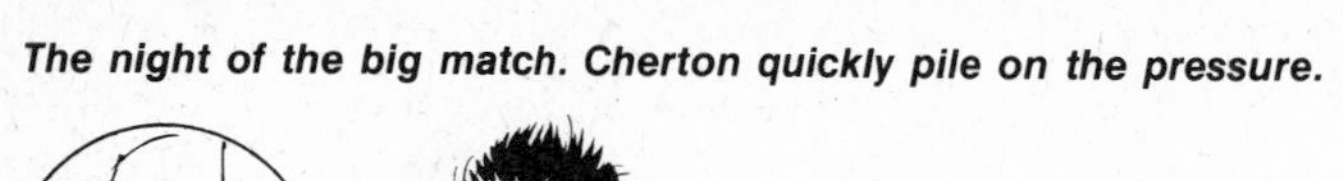
The night of the big match. Cherton quickly pile on the pressure.

They're worrying the defence. That must be about the worst clearance our centre back Bryce Murray's ever made.

GOAL!
CHERTON
THE FIRST GOAL FOR CHERTON! Stark and his men are about to discover how real pros can play the game.

Typical mercenaries! So busy arguing about the first goal, they nearly lost a second!

Stark moves back to sweeper.
Nice one, Jon. We're beginning to get it together.

And ten minutes into the second half . . .
THE EQUALISER! Caught the 'keeper napping there.

Cherton are determined to snatch the lead again. That was a great save by Kevin!

Then with minutes to go . . .
GREAT GOAL, COSMO!

Full-time! It's 2-1 for Weedilstone.
A fluke, Stark! You've made a mockery of English football, but you're going to get chopped down to size . . . AND SOON!
Could be. Porton Villa, the F.A. Cup holders, have just accepted my next challenge . . .

The following Wednesday, fifty thousand fans pour in to see the Porton match, but well into the second half there's still no scoring . . .
Time's running out – and we've got to win, otherwise our plan won't go any further.
Okay, Johnny. He's mine.

AAH!

From the free-kick . . .
That side-on pass by Stark has caught 'em on the hop.

A GOAL!
A fantastic move — from a fantastic game! 1 - 0 to Weedilstone!

And with minutes to go . . .
NUMBER TWO! THEY WON'T CATCH US NOW!

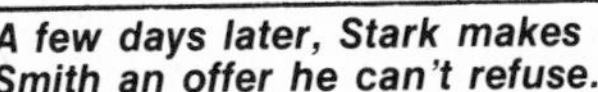
A few days later, Stark makes Smith an offer he can't refuse.

You mean, if the English international team beats or draws with the mercenaries, you'll all retire from football completely? . . . I . . . It's a deal.
Jon's taking a big risk. He's putting us just where Smith wants us. If we lose this match we're out of football for good!

But on the day before the England match comes big trouble.
Kevin would've got to that shot no bother normally. Looks like he's going to be the third player to go down with the 'flu.
We'll just have to use Brian Scott, the young Weedilstone 'keeper and two of his team-mates. It's the only answer.

Next day, Wembley . . .
What chance have we? We're playing one of the best teams in the world with two part-timers and an inexperienced 'keeper . . .
This is where you eat your words, Stark — and I'm going to enjoy every minute of it.

Young Brian fumbles his very first shot . . .
Crikey! Talk about butterfingers!

GOAL!
All they've got to do is keep sniping. We don't have a dog's chance!

Those two Weedilstone players are hopeless, Jon!
Criticism's easy, Cosmo. We've got to give them time to gain confidence.

But England score two more goals in quick succession!
It's the end of football for us for all time if we don't do something fast, Jon.
I'll move into midfield, Bryce. Could be our only chance of swinging the game our way.

It's a gamble! But we're starting to control the game and bring in the part-timers when it is suitable.

Minutes from half-time, Stark unleashes a trick shot, and . . .
GOAL!
That goal keeps us alive – and it makes their goalie look stupid. Brian will have more confidence after seeing a top class 'keeper make such a terrible blunder.

Second half . . .
COVER STARK!

ANOTHER GOAL! Come on, you fools. Stark must be taught a lesson!

But . . .
THREE-ALL! Weedilstone are right back in the game!

England are trying everything to get the winner, but young Brian's more confident . . . and Bryce and the backs are taking the strain.

But we've got to win this game, and this could be our chance. They've pushed too many men forward! So if I hit the ball through . . .

. . . and chase it . . .

IT'S THERE! DONE IT!
MAGIC, STARK! 4-3!

It's the winning goal. After the game . . .
It must be clear to even your dull brain, Smith, that football in England will be a one horse race if the mercenaries play as one team. You'll have to return us to our old status.
Very well, Stark — you win. I'll make the necessary arrangements at the next F.A. meeting.

Thanks, Jon. We don't know how to thank you. Without you, we'd have been finished with soccer for good.
One easy way to pay me back, Kevin . . . just don't save any of my shots next time we play against each other!
THE END

TAKING ON

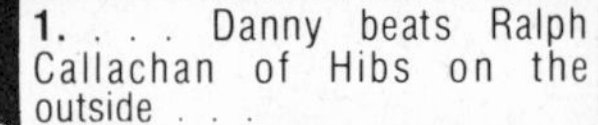

1. . . . Danny beats Ralph Callachan of Hibs on the outside . . .

2. . . . Ally Brazil covering, moves in as Danny feints to the right . . .

5. . . . and lines up to cross into the box . .

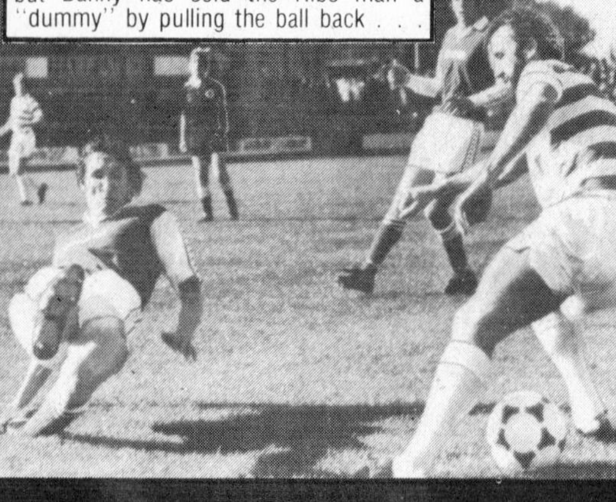

6. . . . Brazil dives to block the cross but Danny has sold the Hibs man a "dummy" by pulling the ball back . . .

9. . . . Danny looks set to cross yet again . . .

10. . . . but instead sidesteps Callachan as he attempts a block-tackle . . .

DANNY McGRAIN

DEFENDERS

Danny McGrain of Celtic is the best attacking full-back Scotland has ever produced. His incredible ball control and change of direction enables him to leave opposing players sprawling in his wake. Our action demonstrates how Danny beats an opponent PLUS the covering defender.

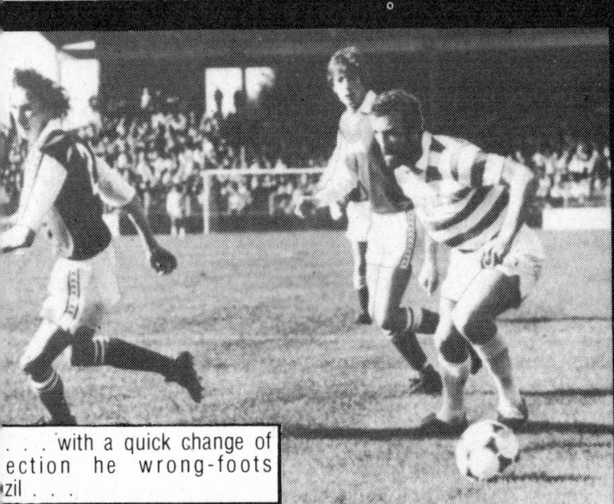

. . . with a quick change of ection he wrong-foots zil . . .

4. . . . Danny now makes for the by-line . . .

. . . Danny now moves ay from Brazil . . .

8. . . . but Callachan is now the covering player and moves in . . .

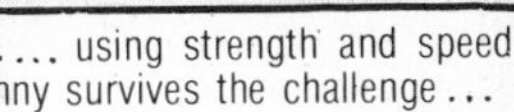

. . . . using strength and speed nny survives the challenge . . .

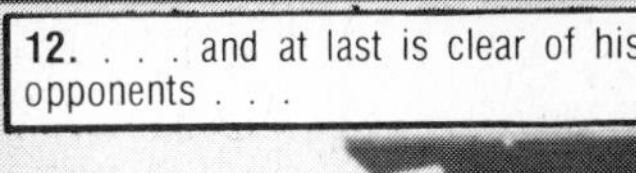

12. . . . and at last is clear of his opponents . . .

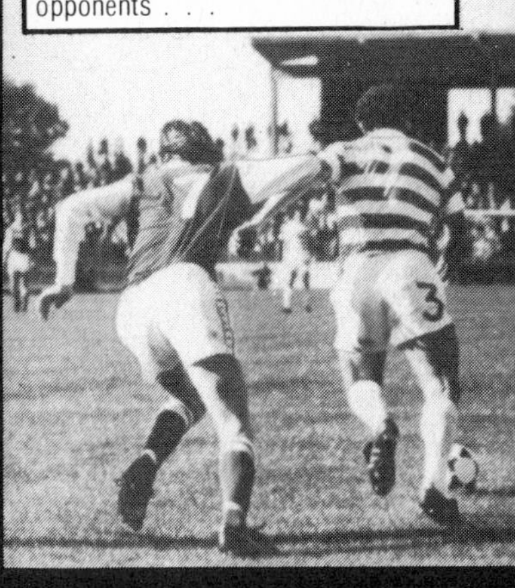

13. . . . Callachan can now only watch as Danny fires in a dangerous low ball into the goal area.

STAR ★ FOCUS

World Champion — FIVE YEARS LATE!

When Jody Scheckter became World Motor Racing Champion in 1979, the only surprise was that he had taken so long to get there! In 1974, his first full season, he finished in third position, and despite securing the runners-up spot in 1977, Jody had never quite fulfilled that early promise.

Not that it was Jody's fault. First the Tyrrell team, then Wolf Racing, just couldn't provide the cars to drive the talented South African to the victories he needed. It was only when Jody switched to the Ferrari stable for the 1979 season that all the expectations of world championship glory were to be met.

Jody had begun by racing karts at the age of 11 and progressed to motor cycles, saloon cars and Formula Ford before working his way into Formula 1 in less than two years, through Formula 3 and 2 racing. This was a remarkable tribute not only to Jody's ability but also to his determination and consistency, two words very important in the Scheckter vocabulary.

As long as that resolve remains, then Jody Scheckter could be around the raceways for many years yet, and more than that — at the top! The years of waiting are over for the champion who won't accept second best.

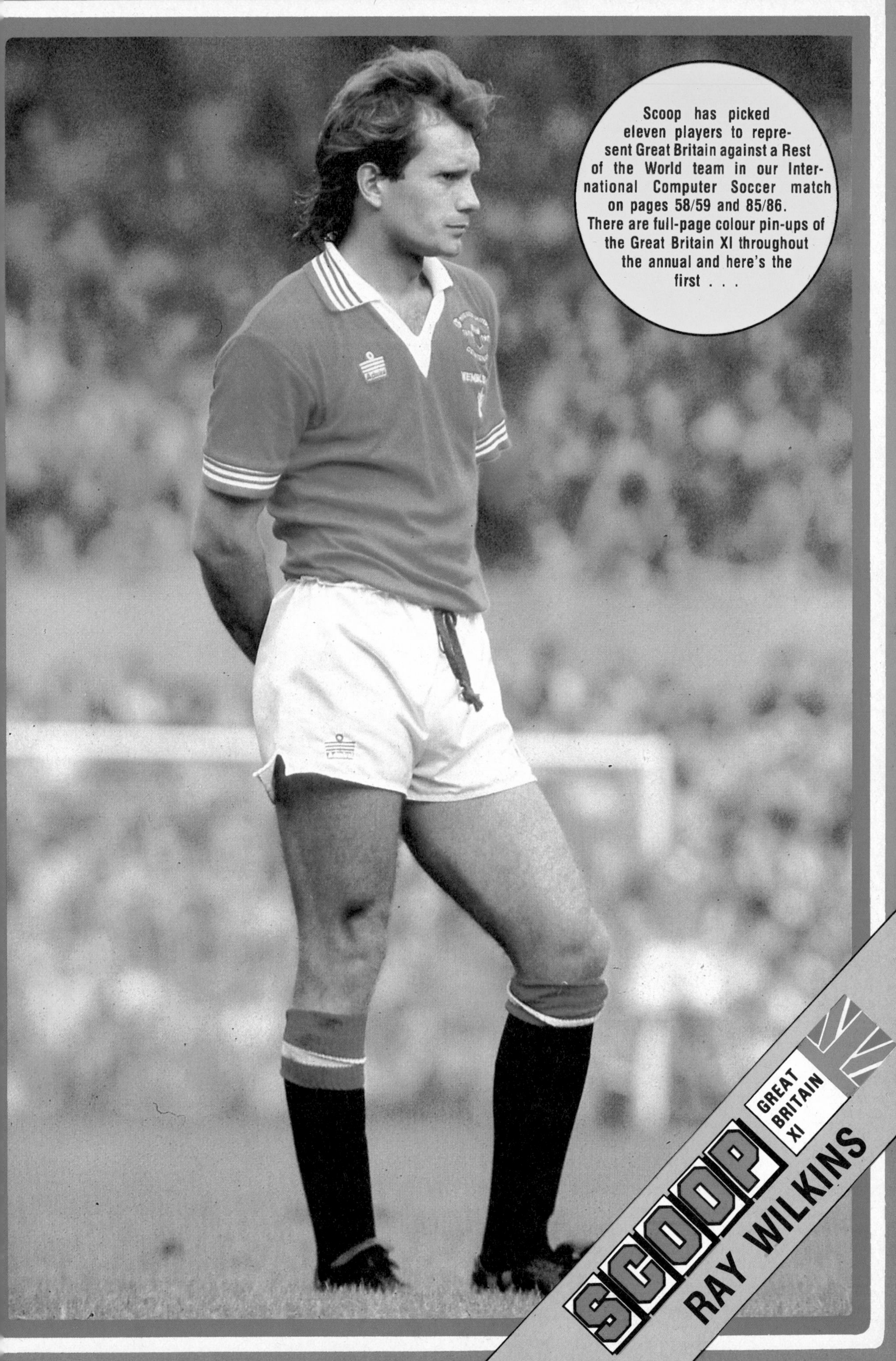
Scoop has picked eleven players to represent Great Britain against a Rest of the World team in our International Computer Soccer match on pages 58/59 and 85/86. There are full-page colour pin-ups of the Great Britain XI throughout the annual and here's the first . . .
SCOOP
GREAT BRITAIN XI
RAY WILKINS

1 Spectacular action as Gilles Villeneuve decides to take a short cut during the Japanese Grand Prix—but, with the exception of pit stops, are Formula 1 drivers allowed to leave the track during a race then return to it?

2 These cycling photographs are pretty similar, but two are identical—which two?

A B C D E F G H I J

3 Mention a photo quiz and Manchester City star Kevin Reeves couldn't resist getting behind the camera as well as in front of it, as he was when he made his full England debut in 1979. But which other player made his full England debut in that game, and can you name the two former team-mates of Kevin who also appear in this pic?

4 By the looks on the faces of these two stars, they seem to be against having their photos in our quiz. Who are they?

6 Here's a mixture from a Spurs-Nottingham Forest clash. If the two players shown were to meet at international level, on a home and away basis, which two stadia would be used?

7 The golfer knocking his hat for six in this picture is South African Gary Player. During 1979 one of his sons broke through into big-time golf. What's his name?

Out for the count, and only the ropes to save this boxer from a tumble out of the ring! But must there always be three ropes in a boxing ring?

8 This wicket-keeper has found an enthusiastic way of stumping a batsman, but if the keeper had been leaning slightly in front of the stumps when the ball was bowled, would the umpire give the batsman "out"?

ANSWERS ON PAGE 89

ANSWERS TO QUIZTIME (PAGES—88-89)

FOOTBALL: 1. Number 2. 2. Home of Lincoln City. 3. Joe Royle (Ha! Ha!) 4. Raymond Neal Clemence 5. Coin, Notebook, Pencil, Red and yellow Cards, Whistle, Watch and Ball. 6. False. 7. Sweden, Italy, France and Tunisia. 8. Sweden. ATHLETICS: 1. The Shot. 2. 800 m., 1 mile, then 1500 m. 3. The starter fires a single pistol shot after the false start occurs. 4. True. 5. Bob Beamon and Dick Fosbury. 6. They're twin sisters. BOXING: 1. Amateur Boxing Association, European Boxing Union, World Boxing Council. 2. True. 3. Cassius Clay (Muhammad Ali). 4. Henry Cooper. 5. Yes, Ken Buchanan won on points. 6. Light-heavyweight. CRICKET: 1. True. In 1805 women cricketers changed from underarm to overarm when the ball kept being caught up in their flowing skirts. 2. Ian Botham. 3. No. 4. Yorkshire and Somerset. 5. Batting, bowling, batting, batting. 6. Surrey. GOLF: 1. Gleneagles, the rest are Open Championship courses. 2. Muirfield. 3. The maximum number of 14 clubs can all be woods if a golfer desires. 4. South Africa, Australia, England and Scotland. 5. False. 6. St Andrews. MOTOR SPORT: 1. Alan Jones. 2. Isle of Man. 3. South Africa. 4. Finnish. 5. Once. 6. Rallying. RUGBY: 1. The name a touring Argentine national team is known by. 2. August 29th, 1895. 3. Jeff Squire. 4. Murrayfield, 5. False. 6. Swansea. TENNIS: 1. It's the world's oldest tennis tournament, dating from 1879. 2. Chris Evert, Billie Jean Moffat and Evonne Goolagong. 3. 1977. 4. True. 5. Bjorn Borg and Roscoe Tanner. 6. Paraquay.

GITANES
Renault
elf
CIBIE
BP
olivetti
BARDAHL
Made in Britain
Shell
NORWISS
elf huiles
PAMPR
ESSO
aseptogyl
MICHELIN
76
20
PAMPRYL
LE VRAI JUS
RTL

LE MANS
FOCUS ON SPEED

For the drivers and the 300,000 spectators who flock annually to the event, the Le Mans 24-Hours Endurance Race is more than just a race — it's an experience never to be forgotten.

This small town in central France which hosts the longest and toughest endurance race for sports cars in the world has become internationally famous since the first race there took place over fifty years ago.

And a test of endurance it most certainly is. For twenty-four hours, the cars, driven by teams of two or three drivers in turn, power their way round the eight-and-a-half-mile Sarthe circuit on the public roads which run through and around the town. Through blistering sunshine or pouring rain, the cars are pushed day and night to the very limit. It's a gruelling test for both man and machine.

DANGEROUS

It also happens to be one of the most dangerous races in the world! Cars of vastly different potential line up side by side, ranging from the dominant works Porsches which can reach speeds of 240 m.p.h. on the Mulsanne Straight, down to private entries which might have a top speed of "only" 180 m.p.h. The problems — hence the dangers — arise in one overtaking the other on the narrow circuit.

It was from just such a manoeuvre that Le Mans experienced its worst moment. In 1955, a three-car pile-up killed over 80 spectators and seriously injured many more as the debris from the wreckage showered down on the crowd, proof that motor racing can be a dangerous pastime on both sides of the barrier. Indeed, at the end of any Le Mans spectacular, the circuit is liable to be littered with cars that have failed to last the course — and it's distance travelled in this 24-hour period that wins Le Mans. The winning car will have travelled approximately 3000 miles — and more cars drop out than finish. The average speeds of around 120 m.p.h. take their toll of even the best cars, and a year's work can literally vanish in a puff of smoke.

PRESSURE

The strain on the drivers is equally heavy. Even during their rest periods, the tension never lets up. Few can relax and it's not all who can live with that sort of pressure. Many Grand Prix drivers, well accustomed to high speeds and high pressure racing, state emphatically their unwillingness to participate — one notable exception, however, being the Belgian ace Jackie Ickx, a several-times winner at Le Mans for Porsche.

Not unexpectedly, French drivers featured prominently when Renault mounted their assault on Le Mans, ending triumphantly in 1978. Depailler, Jabouille, Pironi and Jassaud were the drivers involved, victory falling to the latter pairing, and Renault promptly switched their attention to the GP scene after a long lapse — with ever-increasing success.

Perhaps the most spectacular success in recent years, however, came in 1979, when film star Paul Newman, at his first attempt, and at the age of 54, helped team-mates Rolf Stommellen and Dick Balfour into second place.

For Britain, Alain de Cadenet, who builds and enters his own Lola-powered car every year, and Derek Bell, who seemed set to repeat his 1975 victory in 1977 till his engine spluttered to a halt, have proudly carried the flag.

More than the drivers, more than the cars, though, it's Le Mans itself which is the star of the show. The packed grandstands and enclosures go to provide a carnival atmosphere hard to match anywhere in the world of motor sport.

Worldbeaters!

There aren't many sports where every competitor is a crowd-pleaser—usually there's somebody that spectators take a dislike to; an unsporting tennis player, a wrestler who bends the rules, a footballer who wastes time, a go-slow batsman. Women's gymnastics, though, must be an exception. These teenage girls combine so much skill and technique with sheer effort, that it's hard to take a dislike to any of them. They're never unsporting, never bend the rules, never waste time, and for sheer professionalism, these youngsters could show our footballers and tennis players a thing or two!

Just look at the concentration and skill in this set of pics as these world class athletes tackle the beam exercise . . .

15 YEARS OF STATESIDE SOCCER

When the twenty-four clubs of the North American Soccer League kick off the 1981 season next March, they will be setting out on the league's fifteenth year — a decade and a half which has not only seen the game develop by leaps and bounds in America, but which has come through controversy, tragedy and disappointment — to become a major force in world soccer!

THE BEGINNING

It was in the first few months of **1966** that rumours spread like wildfire through North America about the formation of a professional soccer league. Rumours lead to bitter arguments and in-fighting between several groups of interested parties, but midway through the year, the dust settled and two rival pro leagues emerged — the National Professional Soccer League and the United Soccer Association.

Rivalry was intense, and both bodies rushed to be the first to start playing. The U.S.A. announced that their league would commence in the spring of 1968, yet when they learned that the N.P.S.L. was opening its first full season in 1967, they quickly brought forward their plans. Unfortunately, such was the rush to get the U.S.A. on show, that there wasn't sufficient time to organise its own teams, and whole teams from Europe were "imported" to represent each of its twelve clubs.

The **1967** season ended in turmoil! Though Wolverhampton Wanderers beat Aberdeen 6-5 in a classic game to decide the U.S.A.'s top team, and Oakland Clippers and Los Angeles shared the N.P.S.L.'s laurel wreaths, the season was spoiled by bickering between the two rival leagues. Millions of dollars were poured in by the opposite camps in an attempt to make one league better than the other, and much of it was lost. With the N.P.S.L. averaging crowds of 8000, and the U.S.A. only 4000, many of the clubs became desperately close to going bankrupt.

By the end of North America's first-ever season, Stateside soccer was a shambles!

THE N.A.S.L. IS BORN

Something had to be done! Eventually, both leagues agreed to a merger and, on December 5, 1967, the North American Soccer League was born.

Seventeen teams from both leagues survived the merger and in **1968** the N.A.S.L. began in earnest. Although never reaching a great standard, the soccer was a definite improvement on that of the previous year. Atlanta Chiefs, led by Coach of the Year Phil Woosnam, a man later destined to play a major part in the N.A.S.L.'s success story, overcame San Diego Toros in a two-match play-off.

The troubles weren't over, however! Attendances at games averaged around 4000 and yet again clubs were making huge losses. By the end of the N.A.S.L.'s first-ever season, clubs were flocking to LEAVE the league!

By the start of **1969**, only FIVE teams stated definitely that they would be prepared to field teams in the forthcoming season! Things were better by the time the league kick-off came, but there was still an air of despondency hanging over the N.A.S.L. The annual play-offs were cancelled and the championship went to Kansas City Spurs, who had the best record over the term.

Continued on page 26

The brilliant Pele — seen here playing against Miami Toros.

The Tampa Bay 'Wowdies' — just part of their club's pre-match entertainment.

15 YEARS OF STATESIDE SOCCER

THE STARS THE ACTION THE SCENE

Pele — a living legend.

Soccer maestros Joh Cruyff and Franz Beckenba

Steve Hunt in full cry for Cosmos.

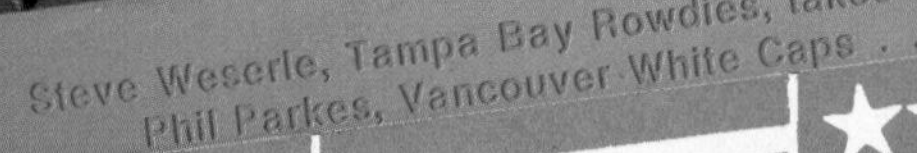
Steve Weserle, Tampa Bay Rowdies, takes on Phil Parkes, Vancouver White Caps . . .

New York Giants Stadium — home of Cosmos.

KICK
Trevor Francis is Detroit's Expressive Wizard
The NASL magazine

The official NASL b

Some of the players meet their fans.

NASL Commissioner Phil Woosnam.

Carlos Alberto. Cosmos.

Johan Neeskens. Cosmos.

... and leaves him for 'dead'!

Action from the 1978 Soccer Bowl Final won by Cosmos.

Tampa Bay Rowdies' Mascot.

The Soccer Bowl trophy.

...oit Express fans welcome ...vor Francis.

Continued from page 23

Lean times continued in **1970** and **1971**. Low crowds, money problems and bad administration combined to make it hard going for all concerned with the N.A.S.L. These two seasons, however, threw up a name which struck fear into the hears of goalkeepers.

The name was Carlos Metidieri, a Brazilian who was affectionately nicknamed Topolino, the little mouse. For both these seasons, centre-forward Metidieri tormented defences all over the continent, amassing thirty-three goals, and helping Rochester Lancers to the N.A.S.L. Championship in their very first season. Metidieri's achievement of being named as the League's Most Valuable Player for both 1970 and 1971 may never be equalled!

COSMOS EMERGE!

Eight clubs lined up for the competition at the start of the **1972** season, and eventual winners were a team which was to play such an important part in the N.A.S.L.'s later years — New York Cosmos! Their 6 ft. 2 in. black striker Randy Horton also picked up the titles of Most Valuable Player and Leading Scorer. The play-off in 1972, between Cosmos and St Louis Stars, also provided what must have been North America's first taste of football hooliganism, when some youngsters threw pebbles at Stars' goalkeeper Mike Winter!

With most teams packed with foreign players, the pride of American coach, Al Miller, was severely dented. So, in **1973**, Al took on the rest of the league with a practically all-American line-up. The result? Triumph! His Philadelphia Atoms team "atomised" Dallas in the play-off final, and Al captured the Coach of the Year award.

Season **1974** brought the N.A.S.L. title to America's west coast for the first time, when Los Angeles Aztecs beat Miami Toros in one of the few top Stateside games ever to be decided by penalty kicks. This was the year that marked the emergence of pro soccer in the West, and Vancouver, San Francisco and Los Angeles themselves put pen to paper to give the N.A.S.L. a total of fifteen teams.

PELE!

Those soccer fans around the world who didn't know much about the N.A.S.L. were about to be blasted with it from every newspaper, magazine and television across the globe. For in **1975**, nearly five million dollars took the legendary Pele from Santos to New York Cosmos.

At the time, everyone agreed that the signing of the great Brazilian was a significant development in the history of the N.A.S.L., but few could have realised what an effect Pele's contribution to the game in America was going to be. He drew record crowds wherever he played, there was a raising of standards in the league as other clubs chased top foreign players to try to compete with the Pele signing, and the exposure and publicity given to the league by Pele's personal appearances, including one at the White House, was immense. Indeed, the word "soccer" was on everyone's lips in America — and that was something that had never happened before!

But even with the great Pele, Cosmos couldn't win the 1975 championship, and the following year, **1976**, they again failed to take the title, despite strengthening their team with the signing of British star Dave Clements and Italian international goal-scoring machine Giorgio Chinaglia. In fact, it was a team inspired by another soccer legend — Eusebio — who won the play-offs. In a final which was to go down as one of the biggest upsets in the American game, Toronto Metros defeated the highly-fancied Minnesota Kicks.

COSMOS COME GOOD

After two disappointing seasons, Cosmos at last won the champion ship, with a 2-1 win over Seattle Sounders in the **1977** Soccer Bov final. However, if there was ever a case of money buying success, the this was it.

As well as Pele and Chinaglia, the Cosmos dollar barons recruite World Cup stars Carlos Alberto and Franz Beckenbauer, and for goo measure, added Stevie Hunt and Yugoslavian midfielder Vitom Dimitrijevic.

Here, indeed, was a team of all-stars, and how well the American publi responded to them. During the '77 play-offs, Cosmos attracted crowds c 77,691 and 74,000 within ten days of each other at their Giants Stadiur home. But how many were there for the soccer and how many were ther just to see the stars? The N.A.S.L. were about to find out, for, at the end c the season a tearful Pele hung up his boots, and his famous No. 1 jersey, for the last time.

Could the N.A.S.L. survive without him . . .?

STRENGTH TO STRENGTH

The answer to the above question was a resounding "yes!" Certainl there was no Pele in **1978**, but they reckoned that there were sti plenty of quality players in the N.A.S.L. to keep the crowds rolling in.

Although Cosmos dominated things yet again, with a 3-1 win ove Tampa Bay Rowdies in the final, a new hero arrived in the shape o Birmingham City's Trevor Francis. And what a capture he was for Detroi Express! Joining them in mid-season, and playing in only ninetee games, the young England star netted twenty-two times — and incredibl scoring rate!

One thing was certain at the start of the **1979** season — the Detroi public wanted Trevor Francis back again. He obliged, and the sta treatment he received came close to that given to Pele in 1975. But it was neither the Express nor the Cosmos who took the last title of the decade The shock troops of that year were Vancouver Whitecaps, and, superbly marshalled by Alan Ball and led up front by the dashing Trevor Whymark, they took the title back to Canadian soil for the first time.

THE FUTURE

So, then, to the present season and the shape of things to come. One thing is perfectly clear — the N.A.S.L. has come a long way since its firs faltering steps. Bolstered by imported players, but not entirely depending on them, it has quietly and steadily set itself the target of Americanising the game. Now these steps are beginning to bear fruit . . .

A new generation of players is emerging from colleges, many of them having come through N.A.S.L. coaching camps such as Tampa Bay Rowdies' "Kick in the Grass" scheme. By the mid-Eighties, we can expect to see only two or three foreign players per team, much the same as many European countries. By 1985 also, we can expect to have a much better idea of how the United States' National team is shaping up. Many home-grown players have already toured the world with clubs such as Cosmos, and, with this experience, will soon be able to compete in the international arena.

The future will have to bring some changes, however. The shoot-ou and offside laws used by the N.A.S.L. will have to come into line wit F.I.F.A. rules if America is to enter international competition. Vice versa it's probable that many European clubs will follow the example given by American outfits and install the smooth, easy-to-play-on astro turf.

All in all, the future of soccer in North America looks rosy — as long as the game continues to develop at grass roots level. If it does, and there's no real reason why it shouldn't, it won't be long before we're looking at a new name engraved on the World Cup trophy — THE UNITED STATES OF AMERICA!

Action from the 1979 Soccer Bowl

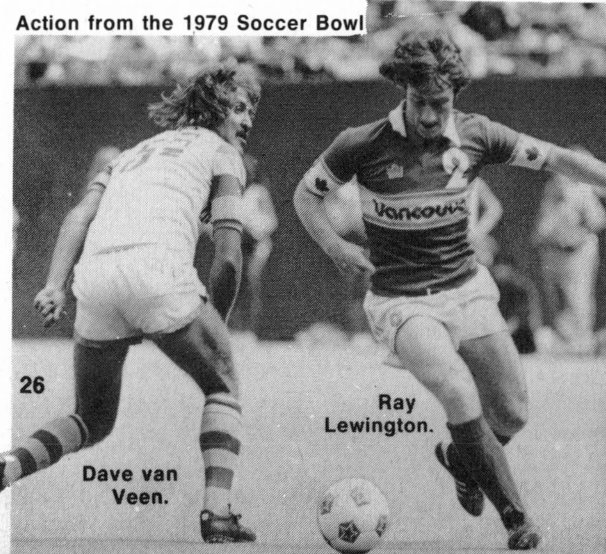

Ray Lewington.

Dave van Veen.

STAR ★ FOCUS

"KILL THE COURSE AND YOU WIN THE OPEN" —SANDY LYLE

. . . the words of a confident and ambitious golfer. And if talent and determination have anything to do with it, Sandy has to be the British golfer most likely to take on and beat the all-conquering Americans at home AND on their own patch!

Ever since he sailed through that tough transition from the ranks of talented amateur to that of hopeful pro, Sandy's looked a real good 'un.

Mind you, he has had a few advantages. For a start, he's been playing the game since he was just three years old. He could hit a drive eighty yards even then!

The game is in Sandy's blood. His father, a golf professional, helped him develop the formidable drive and quality swing that have brought him so much success.

Sandy's first professional victory came in the Nigerian Open in 1978. Since then, he's picked up a very useful collection of wins—including the European Open in 1979!

That Lyle killer instinct should be drawing blood from top class courses for a long time to come.

Look out, Yanks!

Above and below: Two glimpses of the style and determination that make Sandy a star.

THE 4 SEASONS OF SPORT...

4 SEASONS OF THE YEAR AND 4 VERY DIFFERENT KINDS OF WEATHER; AND IF YOU THINK THE WEATHER IS SOMETHING SPORTSMEN CA AFFORD TO IGNORE, JUST TRY PLAYING GOLF ON A SNOW-COVERED COURSE I DECEMBER! WE FOCUS FIRST ON SPORT IN THE SPRING . . . COURSE!

STAR FOCUS

RON HASLAM

Roaring round a track at 150 m.p.h. AND WINNING has been known to make some top motor cycle stars so cocksure and big headed that buying hats can be a problem.

But that's a cap that doesn't fit British sta Ron Haslam. Despite his success since he firs burst on to the racing scene as a fifteen-year-old, Ron's kept his feet firmly on the ground.

And preferably, as far as Ron's concerned British ground. He's never made any secre of the fact that he'd rather do his stuff on the British circuit than on the Continent. It's hardly surprising then that he's always been a big favourite with British two-wheel fans.

Now, though, Ron's ready to stretch his wings and face the world on the race track.

The world had better look out!

CYCLING

The cycling calendar g under way in April. It's stil bit of a cinderella sport in t U.K., but cycling's business in Europe, with pinnacle of the year being famous Tour de France July. The rise in the standa of British cycling over last few years gives re hope for British success

SPRING

GOLF

Golf tees off in
pril, with the usual
ory of bigger prize
oney, bigger crowds
d even tougher
mpetition. The
estion for British
lf fans has to be —
n the giants of the
riving European
rcuit walk tall in
mpetition with the
emingly invincible
nericans?
With Sandy Lyle,
n Brown and Mark
mes in their ranks,
e British must stand
chance!

SPEEDWAY

Speedway action returns to the shale track in March and for the thousands of fans just waiting for the action to begin again, that's good news. Could be good news too for star rider Michael Lee. One of the most talented riders in the world, more success seems assured for the King's Lynn rider.

29

The Mini

WE first heard of the Congoville Giants when they won the championship of All Africa — without losing a match. Admittedly, football in Africa isn't of a tremendously high standard but, with smaller countries continually doing well in the World Cup competitions, it hadn't taken F.I.F.A. long to introduce a World Club Championship — a championship which brought together the champions from every continent of the world.

The final of this tournament was still contested between the champions of Europe and South America, because teams from the other continents just weren't good enough.

At least, that was the case until the year Brookley United brought the most prized trophy in Europe back to Britain's shores. I was the centre-half in that successful European Cup-winning side. Lofty Lee's the name.

We had two World Cup Championship matches to play, mere formalities we thought, before we could go ahead to play the Uruguayan side that had won the Latin American championship.

We brushed Dynamo Chongjin, a small North Korean team, aside with ease and then were drawn to play the Congoville Giants.

They were something of a mystery side. In fact, they had only joined the Congolese League the previous season, winning both it and their national cup hands down. That had given them a place in the African Cup — a place they'd made good use of.

All we knew about them was their record. On the charter flight into the African interior we looked over the statistics again. In the league they had played 24, won 22, drawn 2, lost nil, scored 76 goals for and conceded only 23. Their scores in the African Cup were just as dramatic. They had beaten the Ugandan champions, for instance, 18-0 and had knocked out a Ghanan team by twenty-odd goals!

LITTLE BIG MEN

CONGOVILLE Airport was a strip of mud about as wide as a garden path and we landed bumpily, grateful to be there in one piece.

It was like stepping into an oven, so hot that every breath was a gasp. Congoville lay spread before us, a mixture of mud huts and corrugated iron, steaming silently in the sun.

Maestros!

We'd been airborne for nearly fifteen hours in all and were so tired that we went straight to our hotel. It turned out to be a rather grand, two-storey mud hut in the town's only street. Nobody seemed excited at having the champions of Europe in town and in that heat you couldn't blame them.

The match, the first leg of the semi-final of the World Club Championship, was due to begin at 8 a.m. the following day, before the worst of the heat, a special concession for us.

We got to the ground with plenty of time to spare. We hadn't had much sleep but the sight of the ground soon woke us up! There was no hope of grass growing in that sun, but the mud had been churned up in past matches, then baked rock hard. It looked like a relief map of the Himalayas.

The stands consisted of a few wooden benches stacked on top of each other, and two or three hundred keen fans had got out of bed early enough to take their places. That was when we began to realise why the Congoville Giants had won their home games.

We changed into our strips and strolled out into the sun-light. No-one felt like running about before they absolutely had to and for some minutes there was no sign of the Giants. Then, led by their goal-keeper, they came trotting out.

I don't know who had named them the Congoville Giants because what no one had told us about them, what no one back in Europe had known, was that they were — pygmies!

They came from a village some miles away in the jungle and had, it seemed, been taught the game by a Belgian missionary!

The goalie was a positive giant at four feet nothing. The rest of the side ranged between three feet nine and three feet eleven. They looked like a school under-twelve side!

We were amazed that this team of midgets had taken on all Africa and beaten them — decisively, too. We began rubbing our hands, thought of the sophisticated skills of European soccer, and pictured a scoreline of 36-0.

Two minutes after the kick-off we were two goals down!

The little striker had won the toss and, from the whistle, passed neatly to his left-winger. He could run like a whippet, and shot off down the middle of the pitch with the ball obediently at his feet. Our right-back, Ballard, moved into the tackle and was left standing.

I went forward, determined not to be beaten, but he nipped around me and side-footed the ball lightly but accurately past our stranded keeper!

Seconds later they repeated the move down the right flank!

Two-nil down, we snapped out of our shock and improved a little but at every turn we were hopelessly outplayed.

It wasn't long before their striker added a third goal, making me look as mobile as a beached whale in the process!

We got a goal back early in the second half but finally trooped off losers by 5 goals to 1, with our hopes of a place in the World Club Championship Final as dim as a cloudy night in Yorkshire!

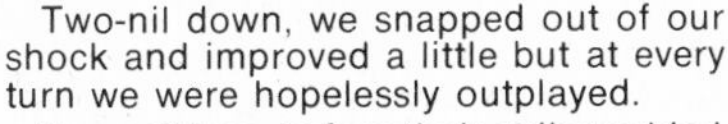

ANOTHER GIANT TEAM

HARDLY anyone spoke on the long plane trip back to Brookley. We were glum, for our chances of pulling back that four-goal deficit on our own ground looked slim.

Only our manager Ernie Enfield looked anything less than suicidal as he occasionally glanced at our red-headed striker Pete Hadden and looked thoughtful.

We didn't know what Ernie and the board of directors had planned for the second leg because we didn't think it really mattered. It would be the Congoville Giants and not Brookley United who would pack their cases for a trip to Uruguay.

The second leg was still a fortnight away when I was called to the dressing-room during a training session. With no explanation I was asked to stand against the wall while the physiotherapist measured me. I'm six feet two, and Ernie looked at the measurement, pursed his lips and nodded.

The Brookley team that lined up against the Congoville Giants for the return match included eight changes. Only Hadden, Smith and myself were kept from the team that had lost.

In the number nine shirt was Ian Napier, the six-feet-four-inch-tall forward who'd come from Westbourne Wanderers. The right-half topped six feet three and had been promoted from our second team. The wingers were also over six feet, and they, along with Marner, a giant left-half, had also come from the reserves.

Brookley was fielding the tallest team in the league, every one a giant. Ernie had decided to play the game in the air and it looked ludicrous. Our shortest player was a yard taller than the tallest Congoville Giant.

GOALS GALORE

NAPIER snapped a goal in the opening minutes, nodding in a high cross, and went on to notch up a first-half hat-trick, all with his head.

Early in the second half we built up another good attack and this time it was Marner, towering high in the Congoville penalty area, who headed home our fourth goal. We'd wiped out their lead and now we needed just one more goal to give us a passport to Uruguay!

Getting that goal was far from easy, however! Each time we worked up an attack, the ball, at some crucial point, fell low enough for one of the speedy Congoville defenders to intercept. Then we had to throw everything back into defence to stop them scoring.

It was from just such a breakaway that the Giants did, in fact, score.

I had dropped back as their left-winger approached, and it looked as if I had him beaten. The left-back was covering the ground to my left, and Marner was backing up on the right. The pygmy couldn't nip past me, and he couldn't go through me.

His flashing feet twinkled and next thing I knew he hacked the ball between my legs — and dived through after it! From that range he couldn't help but slip the ball past our 'keeper for a goal!

We had to throw everything into attack. Minutes ticked away, and there were only ten left when Napier got his fourth, heading high into the net where the goalie couldn't have reached it without a step-ladder. We were 5-1 up, but we needed another if the result wasn't to depend on penalties.

Whether by accident or intent, their right-back tripped Marner inside the box in the last minute of the match. The referee gave a penalty. Hadden placed the ball on the spot and called me over.

I had all the time in the world. The game wouldn't get re-started, it was literally the last kick of the match.

It took me twenty seconds to decide where to put the kick . . . straight for the goalkeeper. He took the ball but, just as I'd reckoned, my kick was so powerful it took him into the back of the net! I knew if I aimed to one side he might have tipped the ball round and if I'd tried for the safe area towards the top of the goal it may have hit the cross-bar or gone over. Scoring a goal with the goalkeeper was a safest shot I could make!

We didn't have any trouble at all winning in Uruguay and so Brookley were the World Club Champions — but it was the tiniest team in the world that had come closest to stopping us!

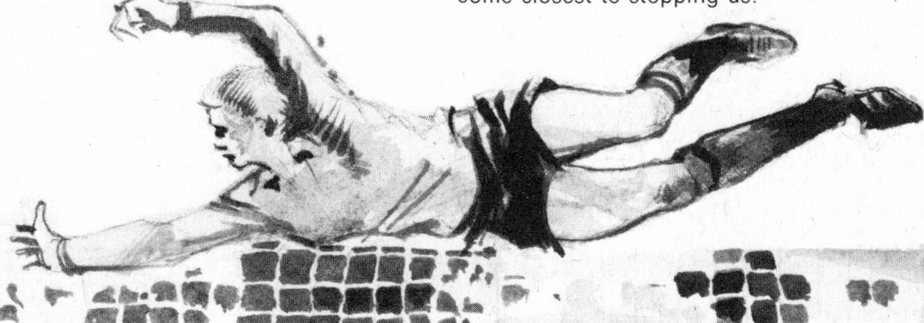

SCOOP
JOHN ROBERTSON
GREAT BRITAIN XI
FOREST FOOTBALL LEAGUE CUP FINAL 1979

TOMMY'S TINY TEAM

It's the final of the British section of a World Table Soccer Tournament sponsored by Hit-Rite, and Tommy Tinman is playing brilliantly . . .

THAT MAKES IT 4-1! THERE'S NO WAY HE CAN STOP ME NOW!

Mr Bollinger, owner of Hit-Rite, presents the prize . . .
HIT-RITE
Well done, Tommy. This is my son David, he's mad keen on table soccer. We'd like to wish you luck for the world finals in Italy next week.
Thank you, Mr Bollinger.

On Monday at school . . .
HE IS THE CHAMPION!
WE'RE GOING TO WIN THE WORLD CUP!
I've not won it yet, lads!

Tommy trains hard at home . . .
I leave on Friday and I've got to be in shape. I don't want to let anyone down!

On Friday, at the airport . . .
Hi, Tommy . . . I'm Jack Fisher, your guide and manager.
Great to meet you, Mr Fisher!

Mr Bollinger and his son are coming over on the next flight, Tommy, so you'll not be without support.
That's great! I can hardly wait for the finals to start!

Two hours later at Rome airport . . .
Here he comes.

Minutes later . . .
TAXI!

TOMMY!
WAAAH!

LET ME OUT!
SHUT UP, BRAT!

AAAAH!
That should loosen his grip!

Tommy seizes his chance . . .
OOOF!

Tommy! Are you all right? We'd better inform the police!
I've given my hand a knock but it'll be okay!

Next day, in the heats . . .
My hand's quite swollen and sore . . . but it could be worse. I'll just have to do my best!
WORL
CHAM

Tommy's best is enough, he wins several heats . . .
2-1 TO ME! IF I CAN HOLD ON, I'M IN THE SEMIS!

Full-time . . .
I'VE DONE IT!

Later . . .
I thought Mr Bollinger and David would've been here to see me. They —
OH NO! LOOK, TOMMY!
NUOVA
PARIS MATCH
IL TIEMPO
IL TIEMPO
INTERNATIONAL
SPORTS MILLIONAIRES SON KIDNAPPED AT AIRPORT— HELD TO RANDSOM!

It says 'A taxi drew up and two men snatched David.'
Almost the same as happened to you. I think we'd best report to the police again, Tommy.
EL JOURNO
MILLIONAIRES SON KIDNAPPED

Mr Bollinger and David were to travel in the same plane as us, Inspector, but cancelled at the last minute. I think the kidnappers mistook Tommy for David Bollinger when they tried to snatch him.
Which puts you in a highly dangerous position, my friends. You are the only people who might identify the kidnappers.

I don't see the man among these photographs Inspector Manzoni. And it's almost time for the semi-final.
Very good. We will look at more photographs tomorrow. Meantime I shall escort you to the competition.

The match begins . . .
I can't concentrate. Suppose that man is out there with a gun?

GOAL!
DASH! NORMALLY I'D HAVE SAVED THAT!

It's crazy worrying! Inspector Manzoni is here to protect me. I must concentrate!

I'm steadying up! Long left swerve.

GOAL!
THAT'S BETTER!

By the end of the game, Tommy wins 3-2 . . .
Well done, Tommy. I'll see you tomorrow!
Thanks, Inspector.

Next day . . .
Perhaps you'll recognise the kidnappers in our files today, Tommy!
I hope so, Inspector.

But suddenly . . .

CRIKEY!
DOWN, EVERYBODY!

GOOD SHOT, INSPECTOR!
AAAAH!

One of the villains makes a break for it . . .
I'm going to help the Inspector!
COME BACK, TOMMY!

He's hiding. I'll get a better view from up here.

There he is! About to surprise the Inspector.

GOT HIM!
WAAAH!

Bravo, Tommy. You saved my life. He'll soon tell us where David is.

Great, Inspector. The quicker we find him the better.
But I've hurt my hand again.

One of the villains revealed David's whereabouts to the Police and . . .
I don't know how to thank you, Tommy. I just hope you win today.
My Italian opponent hasn't been beaten in his last two hundred games— So cheer all you can, David!

Tommy wins the toss and . . .
I'll catch him napping!

AAAAH! MY HAND!
GOSH! HE MISSED BY A MILE! SOMETHING'S WRONG!

A minute later . . .
There's no feeling in my hand. I'm going to lose . . . unless I use my left hand.
GOAL! BRAVO, ITALIA!

In the second half, the score is still 1-0 . . .
It's just as well I practised with both hands.

THAT'S THE EQUALISER!
GOAL!

With seconds to go . . .
The ball is trapped inside a ring of his players but I could use a boomerang shot without fouling them . . .

I've done it and I'm in the clear!

GOAL! GOOD OLD TOMMY!
THAT MUST BE THE WINNER!

It was!
ENGLAND
Gee, I've done it! And boy, am I going to have some story to tell my pals!
The End

SPORTS CROSSWORD

Geoff Boycott is one of 27 across.

A big-hitter in the 50's but what's his surname? See 16 across.

The first name of this superb speedway rider. See 5 down.

Across.

1. Scottish striker, Joe . . . Be careful here! (6)
4. Sure-fire success (3, 3)
9. A player will do this after scoring (7)
10. A draw ----- a point for each team (5)
11. A football boot has one (4)
12. Used for training on the beach? (8)
15. Part of a Midlands team (5)
16. " Slamming Sam," the veteran golfer (5)
21. Trouble with the fans at football matches (8)
23. Mark of a cartilage operation (4)
25. We play them in the Ryder Cup (5)
27. The first two batsmen (7)
28. A spectacular kind of header (6)
29. A footballer is one (6)

Down.

1. ------ Solomon. An American tennis star (6)
2. Some of them come good (7)
3. A tremendous game might be called this (4)
5. --- Olsen, Speedway star (3)
6. There's a famous Olympic one (5)
7. Shoved (6)
8. A team-race (5)
13. ---- Park. The home of Dundee F.C. (4)
14. Jacklin's first name (4)
17. You need a bow and arrows for this (7)
18. The Dutch Master (6)
19. Royal race meeting (5)
20. A superb, coloured French player (6)
22. Troublesome condition for golfers (5)
24. Some clubs must do this to survive (4)
26. --- bin. Used in ice-hockey (3)

ANSWERS

ACROSS.
1. HARPER. 4. HOT TIP. 9. REJOICE. 10. EARNS. 11. LACE. 12. SANDSHOE. 15. ASTON. 16. SNEAD. 21. ROWDYISM. 23. SCAR. 25. YANKS. 27. OPENERS. 28. FLYING. 29. PLAYER

DOWN.
1. HAROLD. 2. REJECTS. 3. EPIC. 5. OLE. 6. TORCH. 7. PUSHED. 8. RELAY. 13. DENS. 14. TONY. 17. ARCHERY. 18. CRUYFF. 19. ASCOT. 20. TRESOR. 22. WINDY. 24. SELL. 26. SIN

It's a funny game, RUGBY!

It can be rough, it can be tough — but rugby can have its lighter moments, too. Some are unintentional, some are deliberate, but they all help provide entertainment for fans and players alike. See if you don't agree . . .

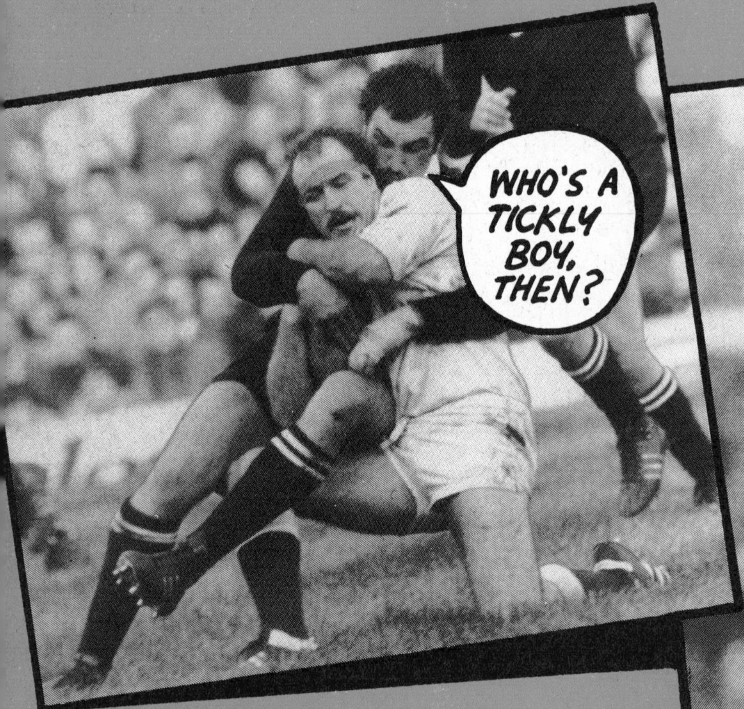

WHO'S A TICKLY BOY, THEN?

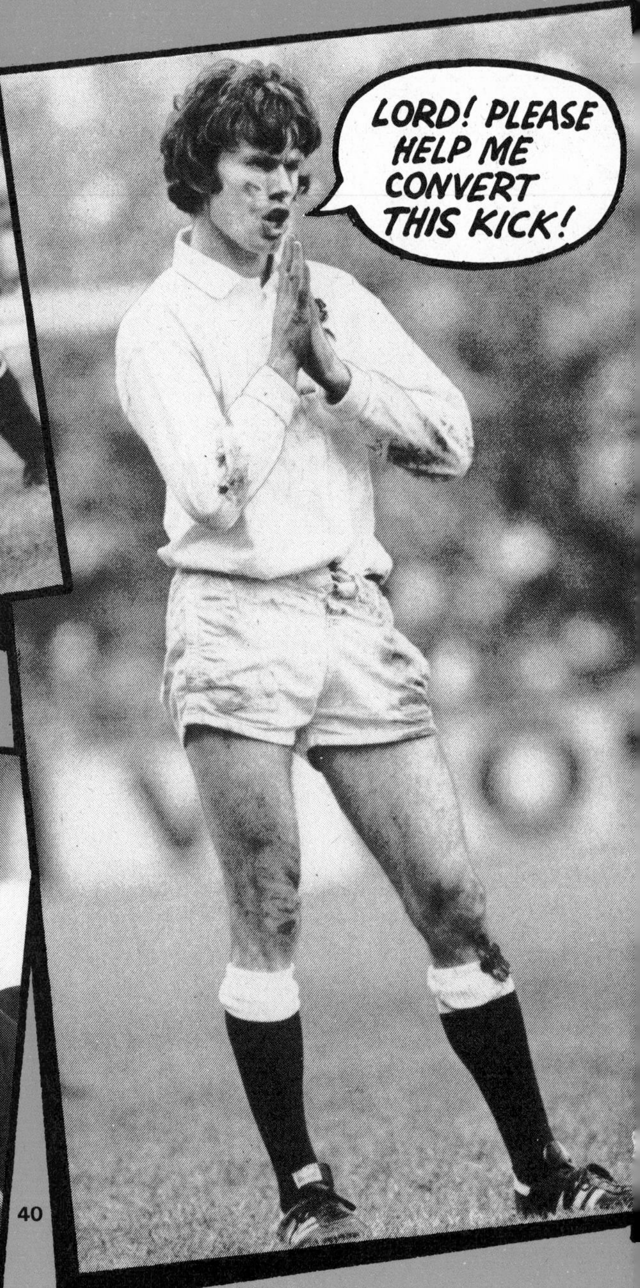

LORD! PLEASE HELP ME CONVERT THIS KICK!

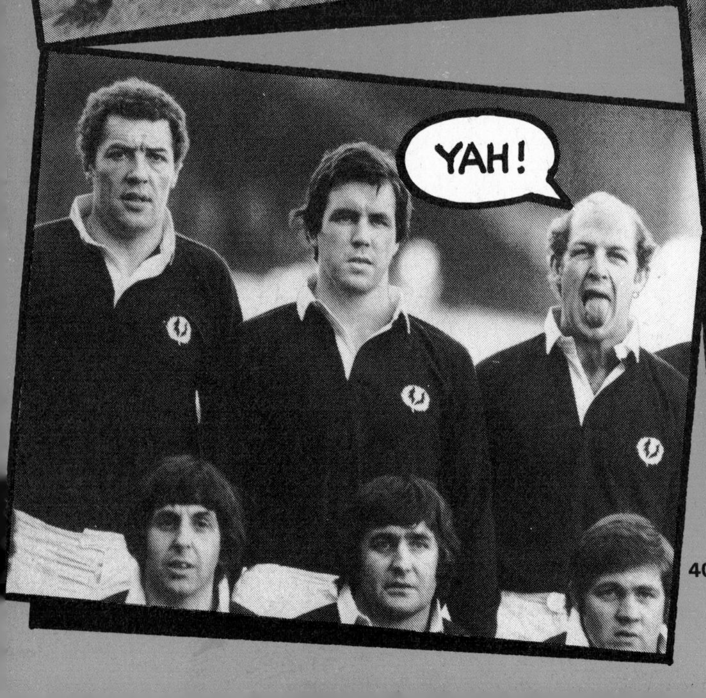

YAH!

NEXT ONE TO CALL US THE NOLAN SISTERS GETS FILLED IN!
OI! QUIT THE KISSING, YOU TWO! THIS ISN'T A FOOTBALL MATCH!
YOO HOO, MUM! HERE I AM!
UESS WHO?!
ONE-TWO-THREE...AND AFTER A FOLDING SHOULDER PRESS, THE FIRST PIN-FALL GOES TO SCOTLAND!

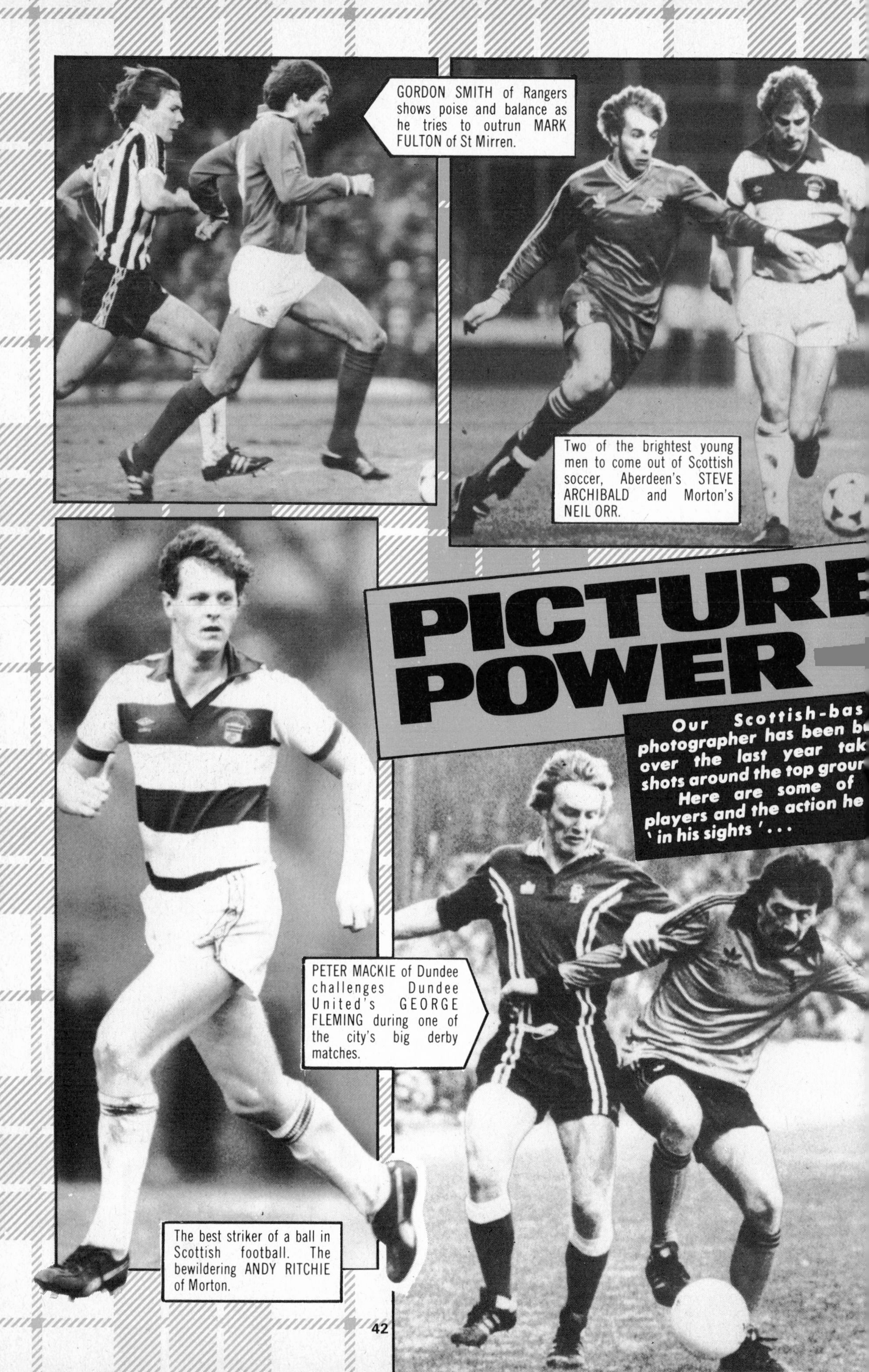

GORDON SMITH of Rangers shows poise and balance as he tries to outrun MARK FULTON of St Mirren.

Two of the brightest young men to come out of Scottish soccer, Aberdeen's STEVE ARCHIBALD and Morton's NEIL ORR.

PICTURE POWER

Our Scottish-bas photographer has been b over the last year tak shots around the top grour Here are some of players and the action he 'in his sights'...

PETER MACKIE of Dundee challenges Dundee United's GEORGE FLEMING during one of the city's big derby matches.

The best striker of a ball in Scottish football. The bewildering ANDY RITCHIE of Morton.

TONY HIGGINS (ex-Hibs) now Partick Thistle, shows his delight after scoring.

Probably the best comeback man of the last year was Celtic captain DANNY McGRAIN. He recaptured his old form and made a welcome return to the Scotland team.

ALAN ROUGH of Partick Thistle is surrounded by players during a Thistle-Kilmarnock encounter.

HITTING THE HEIGHTS!

Pace and agility take Team Fiat star Steve Assinder past Crystal Palace's Richard Rudd.

"Making a basket," it's said, is 40% ability and 60% inches. You can have speed, perfect judgement and the ability to weave your way past players as if somebody has glued their feet to the floor — but if you're not well over six feet tall then you're never likely to hit the heights in basketball.

And certainly there weren't many five footers around when our Scoop cameraman caught some of the action in the Federation Cup Final earlier this year . . .

A rare pause in the action as Team Fiat's Greg White demonstrates the art of shielding the ball.

But at the final whistle it's Crystal Palace who emerge as winners— and doesn't team captain Dan Lloyd know it?

Rebuilt hypertronically after a plane-smash, athlete Ben Norton is also a reluctant agent for the Organisation, a branch of British Intelligence, and is controlled by a pain button if he disobeys orders. During an international athletics meeting in Bulsvakia –
It's my job to play bodyguard to Pavlak – the guy just ahead of me. He's planning to defect to the West. And it looks like my work is about to start – that's a hit-man up there and he's got a bead on Pavlak!
HYPERMAN ON THE RAMPAGE!
PAVLAK! DOWN!
UGH! I – I've been nicked by that bullet.
WHA —!
In a special control-car just a few miles from the stadium, Ben's bosses from the Organisation are watching on audio-visual link . .
Must've been an attempt on Pavlak, Laker, but Norton's on the ball.
Pavlak couldn't be in better hands. Norton's our top man, Alpha — even if he is reluctant to work for us.

I – I feel a bit odd . . . lightheaded . . . I'd better get after that killer – and fast!
Norton! NO! Are you crazy? Leave it to the police!
Must get the killer!
The idiot! If he starts using his super-powers in front of that crowd, he'll blow his cover!
But Ben is filled with an unreasoning fury as he heads for the rear of the stands . . .
He's an enemy — a killer! Those cops are too slow — they'll let him get away . . . Leave him to me!
I'll break him like a straw!
Norton! You fool! STOP!
Say your prayers, you murdering pig!
That leap! You — you're not human!
NOOOOOO! AAAGH!
Norton, get out of there, you idiot — get back to your hotel and we'll contact you later.
What — what happened . . . ? I — I seemed to lose control . . .

As Ben makes his way back to the hotel –
We're losing the audio-visual link with Norton. Something's very wrong here.
We'd better get one of our local men to sort this out!
At the Metropolitan Hotel –
Pain . . . in the back of my head . . . something wrong . . . Bullet must have gone into some vital electronic part in my neck . . . It – it's sending me haywire . . .
Back at the stadium –
That British — Norton — he took out Igor. He must be working for the Organisation!
Then kill him! He's staying at the Metropolitan — Room 304!
But when Alpha's contact man arrives at Norton's room –
Must destroy all enemies — must destroy!
In the name of — ! Norton! What's wrong?
Then suddenly –
Kill them — both of them! We don't want witnesses!
Enemies! Must destroy —
UGH!
AAAGH!
AIEEE!
NUNGH!
In a murderous fury, unleashing every ounce of his super- power, Ben moves in on the three killers . . .

As Ben's blind rage leaves him . . .
Wh – what happened? did – did I do this? I – I don't believe it . . .
Seconds later, alerted by the noise, the hotel manager bursts in with the local police . . .
The man's a maniac! Take him!
Hold it, Mister! Stay cool and come with us.
Oh, no! I'm a dead man if I fall into their hands . . .
If they don't kill me, then Alpha certainly will. He could never allow me to fall into enemy hands and live. He'd use the pain-button to destroy me.
When news of his agent's death reaches Alpha –
That hotel room looked like a bomb had hit it. Norton has run amok. We'd better destroy him — **NOW!**
Do it at once. We have too much to lose.
But, because of the damaged circuitry, the button succeeds only in destroying what little control Ben has over his enormous strength. On the far side of the city –
There he is! After him! Up that fire-escape!
ARRRGH!
AIEEE! He's toppling masonry on us! He's gone berserk!
He's heading off towards the docks now. We'll need reinforcements there.

Seb Coe

As accomplished an athlete as Ben Norton—but without the help of hypertonics—that's Sebastian Coe. Seb shattered the World 800 metre, mile and 1500 metre records in the space of 43 days in 1979 to assure himself a place in athletics history.

Before long –
Got to hide. Mustn't let them catch me.
In Alpha's control car –
The destruct-button hasn't worked! We're still picking up signals from his built-in directional bug!
Then we'll use that to find him. Get a fix on him, Laker. We're going after him!
But the enemy agents are ahead of Alpha and Laker . . .
Norton has been reported heading for the docks. Find him!
We're on our way!
Soon –
Police! No time to argue with them — gun them down!
AAGH!
Meanwhile –
Must reach the water . . . Boats . . . A way home . . .

More of them! More enemies . . . Must destroy them . . .
I'LL DESTROY THEM ALL!
Unable to withstand the enormous impact of Ben's hypertronic fist, the cable and pulley part company, and –
THE CONTAINER — I CAN'T STOP!
KILL! KILL!
YEAARGH!
Look, Laker! There's Norton! Get him before the police spot him.
Just hope I don't miss, sir!
ARRGH!
The police seem to think Norton must have been in that car when it exploded. They won't be looking for him now they think he's dead.
He may be that anyway! And even if the fall hasn't killed him, he'll need immediate treatment.
Later—
He's lucky — just badly bruised. That was a fine shot with the knock-out dart, Laver.
We can repair him and put him back into service. He won't be happy about that . . . but there's no escape from the Organisation!
THE END

THE 4 SEASONS OF SPORT...

TENNIS

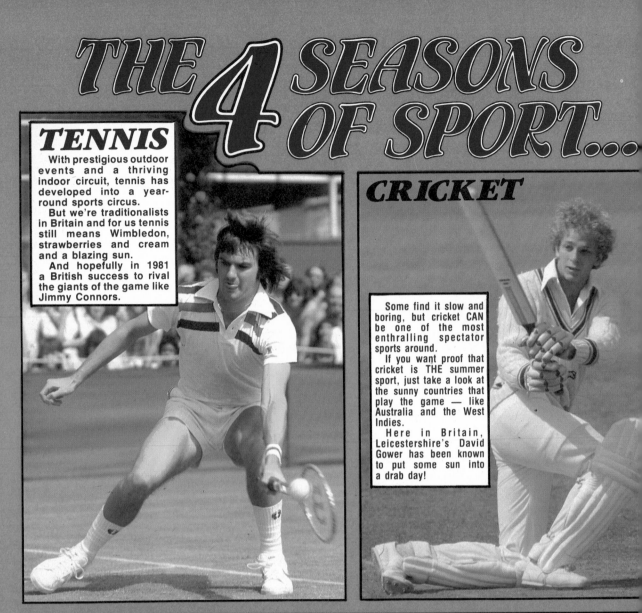

With prestigious outdoor events and a thriving indoor circuit, tennis has developed into a year-round sports circus.

But we're traditionalists in Britain and for us tennis still means Wimbledon, strawberries and cream and a blazing sun.

And hopefully in 1981 a British success to rival the giants of the game like Jimmy Connors.

CRICKET

Some find it slow and boring, but cricket CAN be one of the most enthralling spectator sports around.

If you want proof that cricket is THE summer sport, just take a look at the sunny countries that play the game — like Australia and the West Indies.

Here in Britain, Leicestershire's David Gower has been known to put some sun into a drab day!

HANG-GLIDING

Blue sky, a fresh breeze and plenty of guts, that's all you need to fulfil that age-old ambition to fly.

And when else could you expect to find that perfect hang-gliding combination other than in summer?

SUMMER

ALLAN WELLS

Every summer, railway fanatics flock in their thousands to York Railway Museum to gaze in awe at one of Britain's fastest trains, the Flying Scotsman.

Nowadays, though, if you travel to Crystal Palace or maybe Gateshead, you'll find that Britain has a new flying Scotsman, Edinburgh-born Allan Wells. He's the fastest Briton who has ever lived!

Allan's exploits on the track are legendary. But when he was a schoolboy he had looked a great athletics prospect as a long-jumper!

When he tried to make it at senior level though, he discovered that despite all his efforts he was losing a couple of inches in his jumps every year. In 1977 he stopped knocking his head against a brick wall and switched to sprinting.

Since then, he's sprinted right to the top!

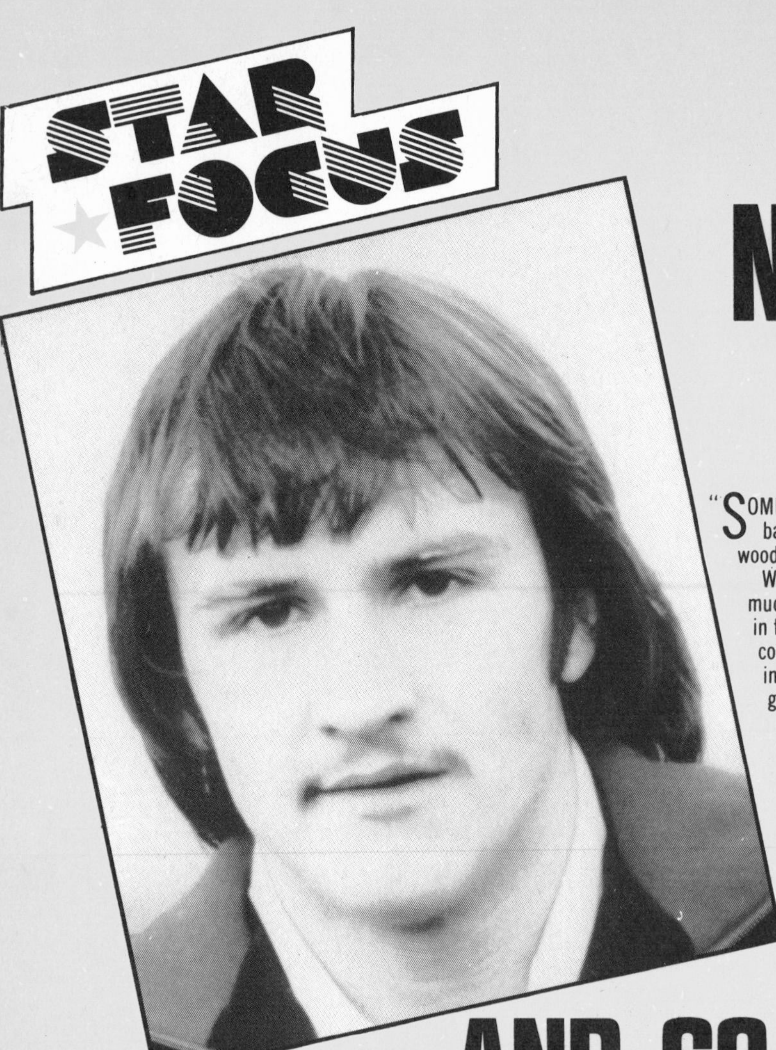

I'M A NORTHERN LAD...

"SOME folk say that football in the North East is a bit of backwater. They reckon that football in this neck of th woods lacks the glamour and style of football further south.

Well, maybe we don't figure in the headlines quite much as other teams but I'm convinced there are playe in the north who are as good as any in any other part of th country. Add to that the fact that the atmosphere at gam in the north is just as needle sharp as at any oth grounds. The fans are as enthusiastic and loyal as any.

Maybe I'm a bit biased. I've played all my footb in the north, first for Middlesbrough, now f Sunderland but there are lots of other players here who stick to Northern clubs. Lads like Stua Boam, Irving Nattrass, Alan Shoulder and Jo Craggs are just some I can name.

Football in the south may have its attractio but I enjoy my football up here."

...AND SO ARE THEY

JOHN CRAGGS (Middlesbrough)

ALAN SHOULDER (Newcastle United)

STUART BOAM (Newcastle United)

IRVING NATTRASS (Middlesbrough)

KLOG
SCOOP'S
STONE-AGE
SOCCER
STAR
HERE COMES THAT BIG-HEADED, LITTLE TWERP OF A WINGER!
SMOOTH GLIDING RUN
MORNING!
ONLY YOU BETWEEN ME AND THE GOAL, KLOG! HOW YOU GOING TO STOP ME, EH? HOW YOU GOING TO STOP OL' TWINKLE-TOES?
TWITCH!
TWITCH!
EASY . . .
CRACK!
. . . WITH A STICK!

SCOOP
GORDON McQUEEN
GREAT BRITAIN XI
MANCHESTER UNI
1878
1978
CENTENARY

MINERVA
GROU
SCOOP
GREAT BRITAIN XI
TREVOR BROOKING

INTERNATIONAL

COMPUTER SOCCER

GREAT BRITAIN v. THE REST OF THE WORLD

HOW IT WORKS.

Scoop reporters Hux and George are the respective managers of Great Britain and the Rest of the World. They pick the teams and the Scoop sports computer plays the game, having been programmed with all the relevant information on the players.

BRITAIN REGRET MISSED FIRST HALF CHANCES!

GREAT BRITAIN: 4-3-3. SHILTON (England); McGRAIN (Scotland), BURNS (Scotland), McQUEEN (Scotland), SANSOM (England); HODDLE (England), R. WILKINS (England), BROOKING (England): KEEGAN (England, Capt.), DALGLISH (Scotland), ROBERTSON (Scotland).

THE REST OF THE WORLD: 4-4-2. HELLSTROM (Sweden): KALTZ (W. Germany), PEZZEY (Austria), TRESOR (France), CABRINI (Italy): MARADONA (Argentina), RUMMENIGGE (W. Germany), PLATINI (France), DIRCEU (Brazil): KRANKL (Austria), KEMPES (Argentina).

VENUE: Wembley Stadium, London.

HANS KRANKL – Quiet first half for the Rest of the World.

COMPUTER READOUT—

Britain kick off on a pitch with a lot of surface water. Robertson breaks down the left and crosses. The ball is cleared easily by Bruno Pezzey.

Hoddle is soon in action when he heads a Robertson cross just over the bar.

In five minutes Dalglish comes close. He is put through by Kevin Keegan and eludes two defenders before ploughing into the box. The ball runs away from him but he stretches and gets in a shot, which hits the post, but Tresor scrambles the ball away for a corner.

Hellstrom easily clutches the resultant kick. The Rest of the World reply when Kempes intercepts the ball in midfield and sends Maradona off down the right. His cross is met by Krankl, but Peter Shilton holds the header.

Dirceu is next to test the British 'keeper with a hard long-ranger.

A pass-back by Cabrini almost leads to a Great Britain goal in 13 mins. The ball is not struck firmly enough and Keegan darts in to shoot. Hellstrom is off his line quickly to dive and smother the ball.

Two minutes later the World win their first corner. It is headed into the goalmouth and Shilton flops on the ball to prevent Rummenigge shooting. A good save.

OFFSIDE

Wilkins cannons the ball off the junction of the bar and post after Brooking crosses, but the linesman has his flag up for offside. Wilkins is in the thick of the action again in the 19th minute when he goes down in the box in a tussle with Kaltz. The referee ignores claims for a penalty.

Moments later Wilkins, yet again, tries to put his side in front when he stoops low to head goalwards, but Hellstrom is well positioned. In 23 minutes, Dalglish forces the Swedish 'keeper to pull off a world-class save. The Liverpool man collects the ball on the edge of the box and looks up before shooting for the top right-hand corner. The goal looks certain until the Swede twists up and back to fingertip the ball over.

The World break out of defence and Dirceu jinks his way towards the G.B. goal. Burns intercepts however and passes back to Shilton.

At the other end Robertson is sent clear down the left wing. He cuts in and shoots, but Hellstrom clutches his effort cleanly.

PENALTY CLAIM

The G.B. team make their second penalty claim on the half-hour mark, when Brooking is felled in the box as he picks up a return pass from Keegan, but again the referee waves away the appeal.

REQUEST BY HUX: PLEASE SHOW VIDEO SCREEN REPLAY OF PENALTY INCIDENT.

REPLAY SHOWS KALTZ MADE CONTACT WITH THE BALL FIRST. THE REFEREE WAS CORRECT.

Sansom is next to try his luck when he fires hard and low but the ball hits the side-netting. Cabrini gets a warning from the ref. for a foul on Keegan. From the free-kick Dalglish gets up well but his header goes over the bar.

Keegan has the home fans cheering in 33 minutes when he gets the opening goal.

Dalglish passes to his striking partner midway in the World half, KEEGAN eludes the tackles of Pezzey and Tresor and then sidefoots home from a narrow angle.

The Rest of the World reply a minute later when Krankl has the ball in the net, but he is ruled offside. Then Dalglish gets his head to a McGrain cross from the right. He heads downwards from close range and the ball beats Hellstrom, but Tresor is there to clear off the line.

The World team almost draw level in 37 mins. There seems to be little danger when Sansom passes back to Shilton. But the England 'keeper slips as he comes out and the ball rolls towards the goal. It hits the post and Shilton is quick to grab the rebound.

Platini tries a snap-shot but is well wide. Maradona follows this by picking up a cross on the edge of the British box and Shilton pulls off an acrobatic save from the shot, which is applauded by the little Argentinian.

Shilton denies the visitors again when he dives to his right to hold a Rummenigge header on the goal-line.

Five minutes to half-time, there's a sensation when Dalglish finishes off a long run with a lob over Hellstrom, who is well out of his goal.

The ref. gives the goal with the World players protesting that the linesman has his flag up.

The linesman is called over and after consultation with him the referee disallows the goal, the reason being that Robertson was in an offside position when Dalglish lobbed the ball!

Two minutes later PEZZEY equalises. The big No. 5 gets his head to a cross from the right and Shilton can only watch as the ball goes in at the top corner.

As the game approaches the interval, McGrain crosses from the touchline but Hellstrom comes out and beats Keegan to the ball.

RAY WILKINS – Looking every inch a world-class player.

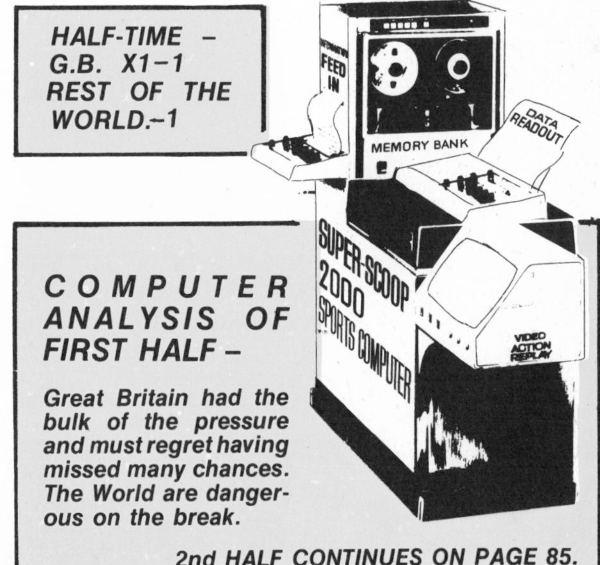

HALF-TIME – G.B. X1–1 REST OF THE WORLD.–1

COMPUTER ANALYSIS OF FIRST HALF –

Great Britain had the bulk of the pressure and must regret having missed many chances. The World are dangerous on the break.

2nd HALF CONTINUES ON PAGE 85.

Life With The Rovers

Whether it's First Division or Fourth, life behind the scenes of a full-time football club follows a similar pattern. It's a side of the game fans don't often see but the preparation and build-up for a match is the same at Belle Vue as it is at Anfield as Scoop discovered when it visited Doncaster

The day before the match, a cup tie against Third Division Mansfield, Rovers' manager Billy Bremner makes a final decision on his team and talks to the local Press . . .

The phone lines in the secretary's office are kept busy, too, as ticket enquiries are attended to . . .

Mid-morning, and it's a last chance for the players to limber up for the following day's match as Boss Bremner puts them through their paces . . .

There's a special training session, too, for 'keeper Dennis Peacock whose task it will be to shut out the Mansfield attack.

Training over, it's time for a final tactical talk while the apprentices, the professionals of the future, clean out the dressing rooms — and still find time for some light-hearted banter.

After a team lunch, the players drift into the dressing-room. Time for a last check on the opposition as the tension mounts . . .

Come match day, club physiotherapist Gerry Delahunt attends to any niggling injuries and packs his bag of medical supplies. The days of the "magic sponge" are long over!

Meanwhile, outside the ground, the crowds begin to gather, with the colours of the local favourites on sale . . .

Three o'clock and the faithful are in their places on the terraces, as noisy and enthusiastic as any . . .

The behind-the-scenes planning now rests on ninety minutes of all-out action — but in this instance there's no happy ending for Doncaster. Mansfield move into the next round of the Cup with a 2-1 victory and Rovers are left to pick up the pieces the following week, planning and preparing for their next match. Life at Belle Vue, as at Anfield, goes on.

The White Water Wonders . . .

. . . . that's the title given to the daredevil breed of sportsmen who hurl themselves down long stretches of river with only a paddle and lightweight fibre-glass shell between them, sharp-edged rocks and thrashing torrents of white water rapids.

It's a testimony to the skill of canoeists and the design of their equipment that very few are either injured or drowned. Little wonder that non-canoeing onlookers, who see them for the first time, shake their heads in disbelief when grinning and unscathed canoeists emerge from a well of water at the end of a course.

But judging by these photos, canoeing CAN have its hairy moments!

the INVADERS

KENNY DALGLISH TALKS FOOTBALL

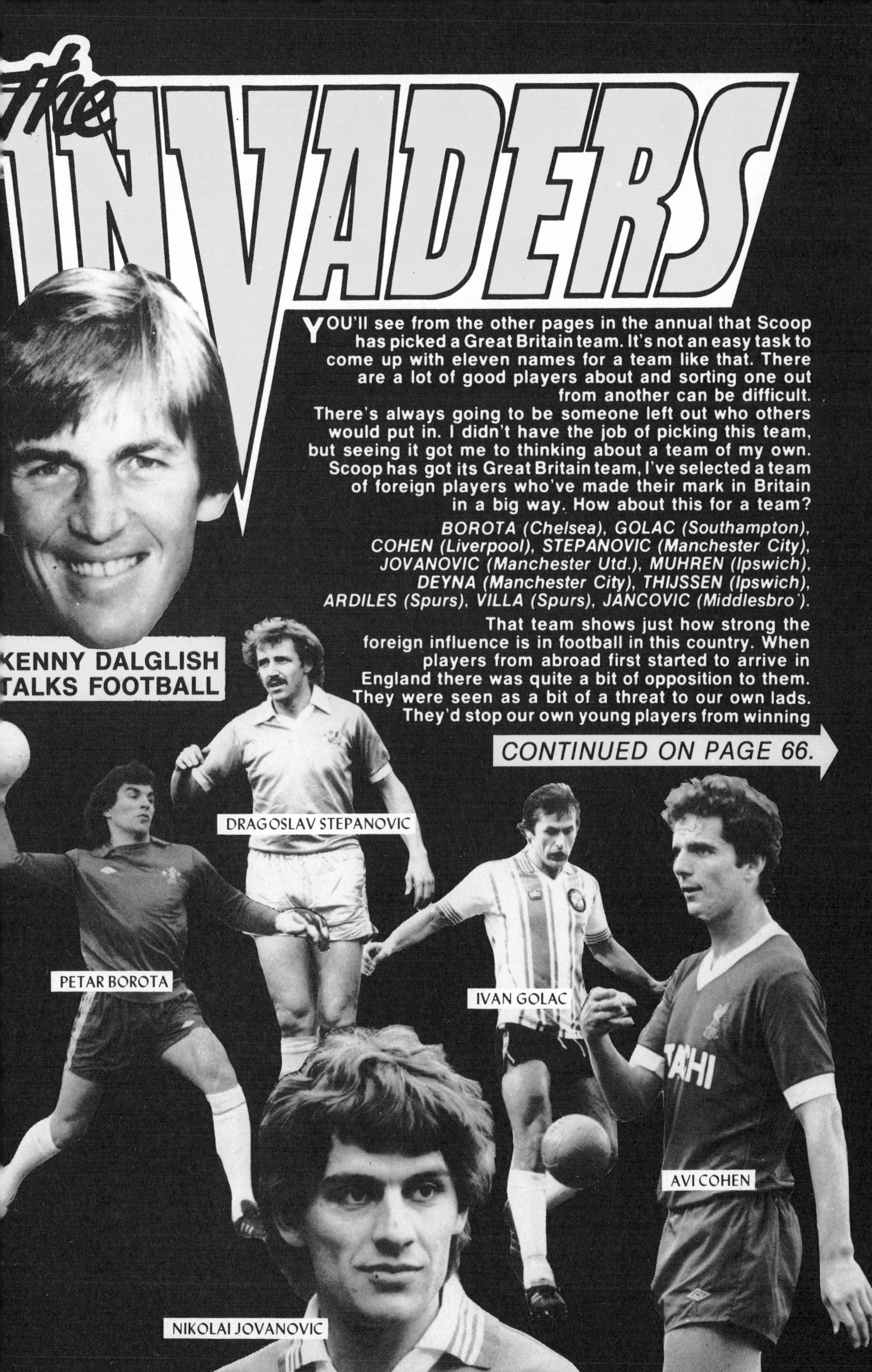

YOU'll see from the other pages in the annual that Scoop has picked a Great Britain team. It's not an easy task to come up with eleven names for a team like that. There are a lot of good players about and sorting one out from another can be difficult.

There's always going to be someone left out who others would put in. I didn't have the job of picking this team, but seeing it got me to thinking about a team of my own. Scoop has got its Great Britain team, I've selected a team of foreign players who've made their mark in Britain in a big way. How about this for a team?

BOROTA (Chelsea), GOLAC (Southampton), COHEN (Liverpool), STEPANOVIC (Manchester City), JOVANOVIC (Manchester Utd.), MUHREN (Ipswich), DEYNA (Manchester City), THIJSSEN (Ipswich), ARDILES (Spurs), VILLA (Spurs), JANCOVIC (Middlesbro').

That team shows just how strong the foreign influence is in football in this country. When players from abroad first started to arrive in England there was quite a bit of opposition to them. They were seen as a bit of a threat to our own lads. They'd stop our own young players from winning

CONTINUED ON PAGE 66.

DRAGOSLAV STEPANOVIC

PETAR BOROTA

IVAN GOLAC

AVI COHEN

NIKOLAI JOVANOVIC

SCOOP
GLENN HODDLE
GREAT BRITAIN XI

SCOOP
GREAT BRITAIN XI
KENNY DALGLISH

THE INVADERS

a first-team place, that was one argume that was put forward. Well, that may certain happen in some clubs, but the your players can benefit as well. The foreig players have a lot of skill and talent and they'v got a lot to teach young player

It's obvious the impact that Ardiles and Villa have had on the style of play Tottenham. The quick one-twos, the close interpassing ar understanding that's the basis of their play is spreading through the who Tottenham team. The same goes for Muhren and Thijssen at Ipswic Their style of play has rubbed off on their team-mates, and I'm sure Ipswic youngsters will learn a lot from playing and training with these tw talented players. Mind you, it's not all one-way traffic. I'm sure the foreig players have learnt quite a bit from playing over here, to New tactics, different ways of taking free-kicks and corners, we can all lea something from other teams and player

The same goes for British players who go to the Continent: Kevin Keegan, Laurie Cunningham and Tony Woodcock, for instance, I'm sure had some tricks of the trade that their new clubmates picked up and learned from. Likewise, players from other clubs and other countries can do a lot to freshen up football here.

And I reckon it could be a good thing, too, for any clubs in Britain who have to play in European competitions. The more we learn about the way other teams play, the better placed we are to cope with them.

No matter where they come from, we need top players of skill and talent.

All the Best
Kenny Dalglish

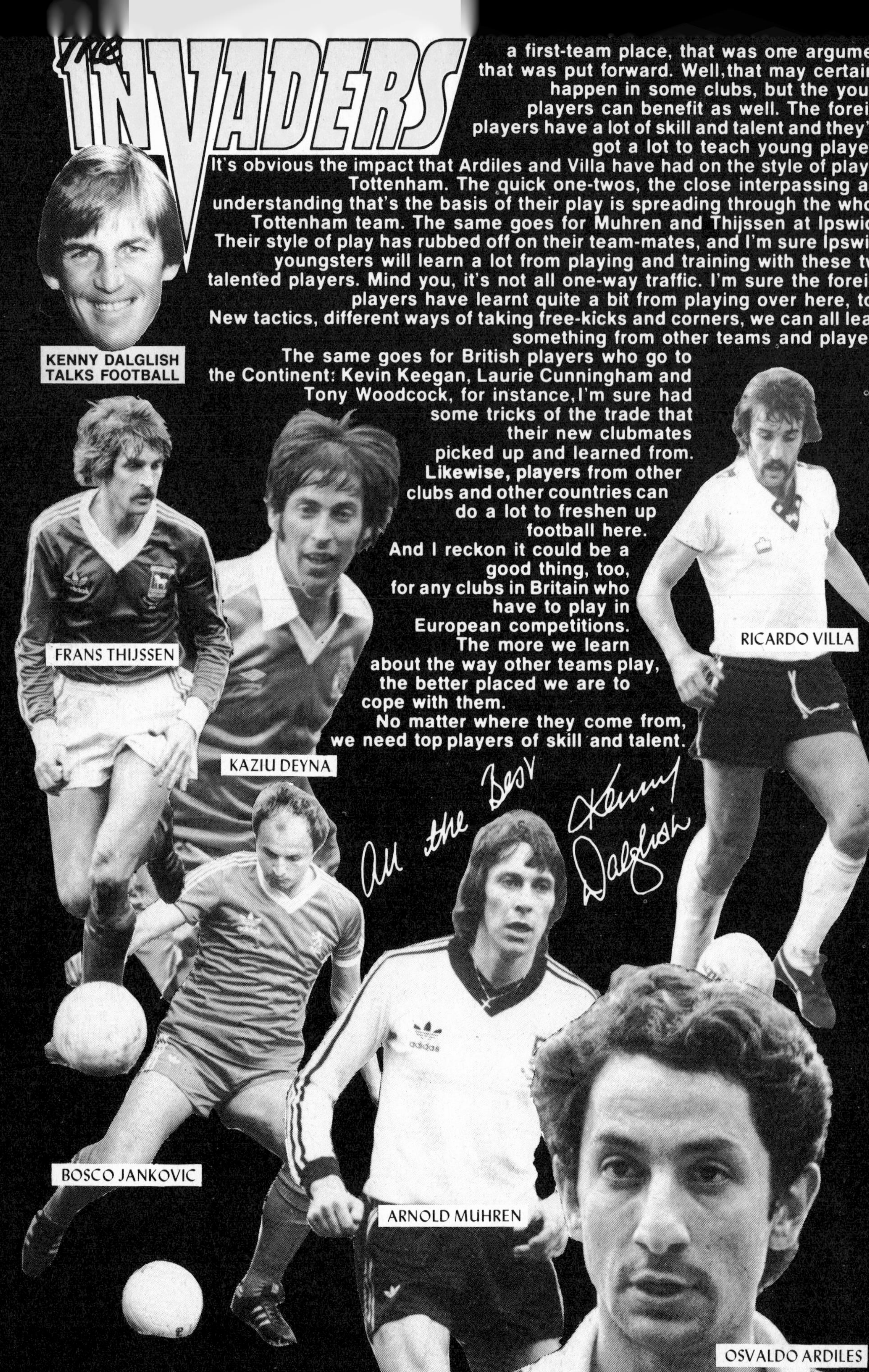

KENNY DALGLISH TALKS FOOTBALL

FRANS THIJSSEN

KAZIU DEYNA

RICARDO VILLA

BOSCO JANKOVIC

ARNOLD MUHREN

OSVALDO ARDILES

★ STAR FOCUS

BATTLIN BOTHAM!

When Kerry Packer took the cricketing world by storm by setting up his world circus in 1977, the English international scene was dealt a severe blow by the loss of players such as Dennis Amiss, Derek Underwood, John Snow, Bob Woolmer, Tony Greig and Alan Knott—all recognised England team members.

Selectors were forced to look around for new players, and one of the first they promoted to the national side was Somerset all-rounder Ian Botham.

Since then, Botham has taken Test cricket by storm! His swing bowling has become feared, his powerful batting has forced fielders to the boundaries.

A new height to his short, but incredibly successful international career, came in 1979 when he became the youngest and quickest player to take 100 Test wickets and score 1000 Test runs.

He followed that up early in 1980 by becoming the first player ever to score a century and take over 10 wickets in the same test.

The making of this star took just two years!

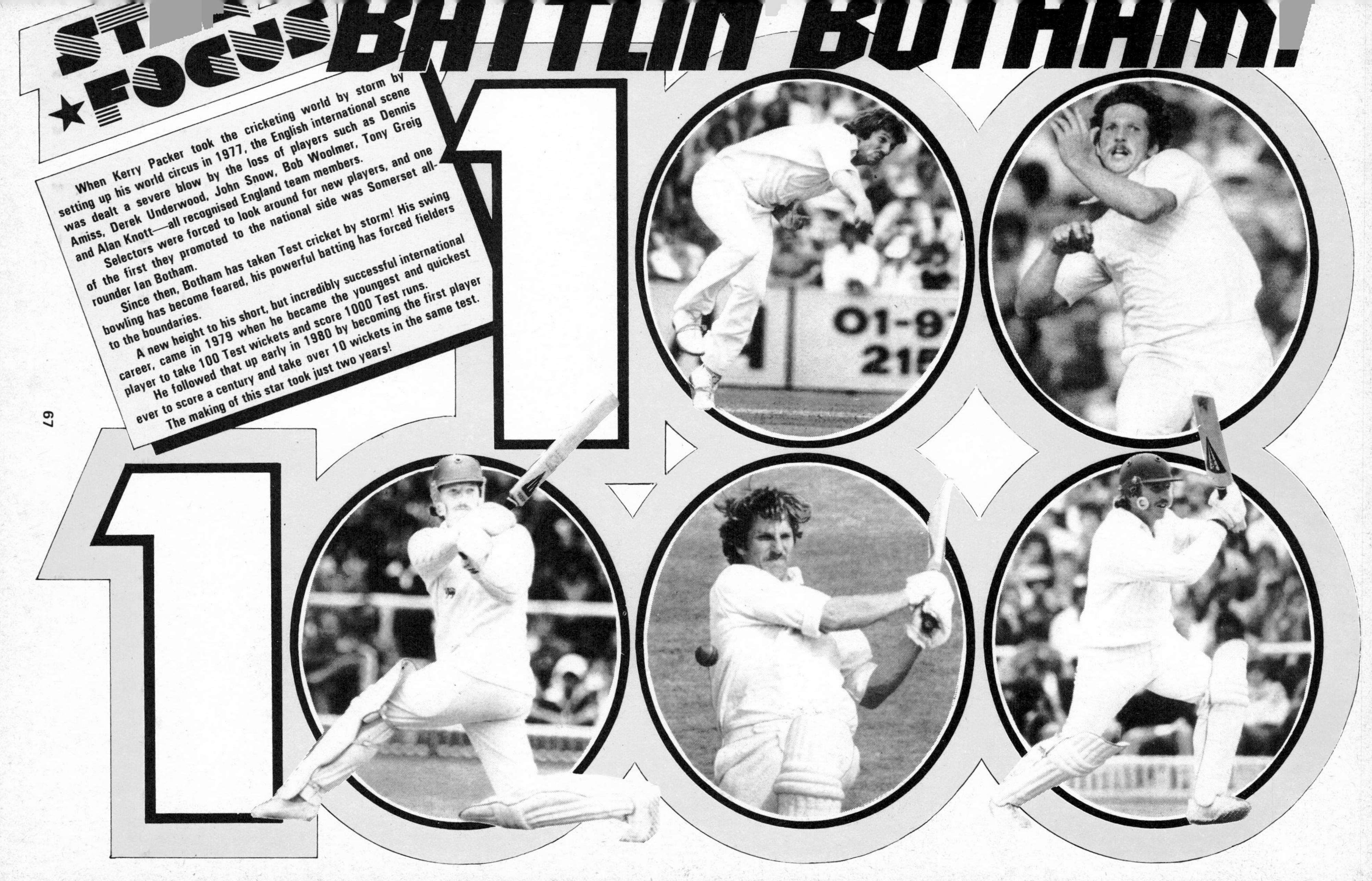

elf
Tyrrell
GOODYEAR
Beta
Renault
elf
copersucar
28
parmalat
parmalat
parmalat
GOODYEAR
GOODYEAR
Labatt
VALVOLINE
GOODYEAR
parmalat
MICHELIN
14
parmalat
parmalat

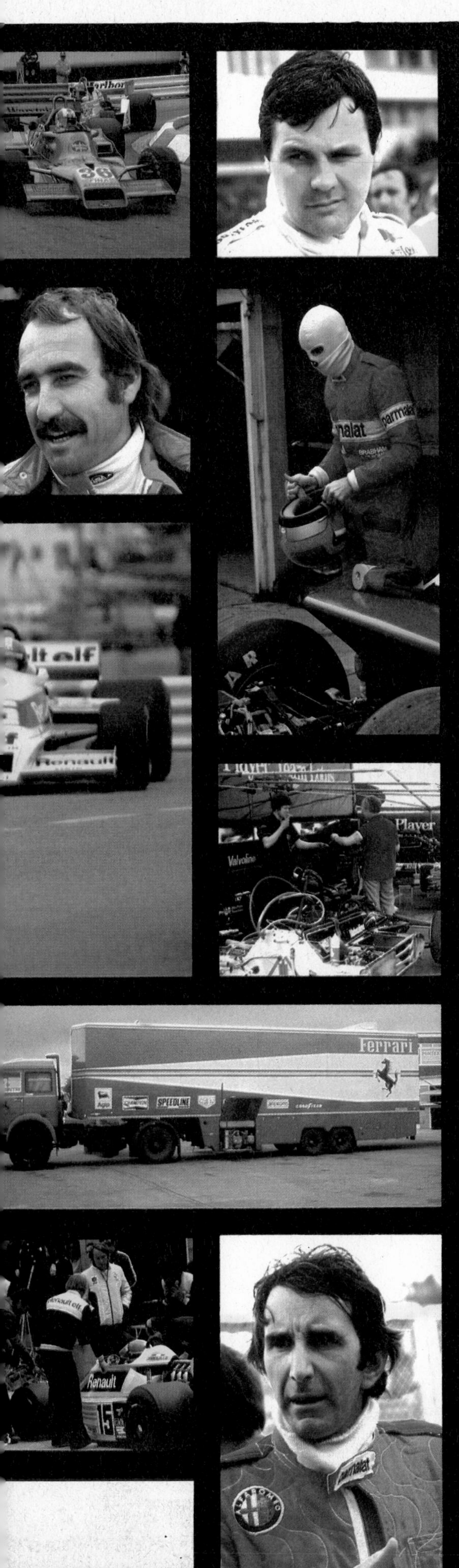

GRAND PRIX

FOCUS ON SPEED

The cars are bigger and faster — but are they any better? That's the dilemma facing Grand Prix racing. For while technological advancements push the cars to limits previously out of reach, many people in the sport feel that much of the excitement of motor racing is being lost.

Modern cars are such highly developed and sensitive pieces of machinery that races are more often than not won on the drawing boards of the designers. The flair and skill of the drivers, though still basic ingredients of Grand Prix, are now being challenged by technology.

Of course, that's not to say that in times gone by the design and behind-the-scenes know-how didn't have a bearing on racing — and winning. But then the outcome of the race depended more on the ability of the drivers.

That's why the names of Ascari, Fangio, Stirling Moss and Jim Clark survive the test of time.

In more recent times, Jackie Stewart and Niki Lauda are among the few who have been able to stamp their own personalities on the scene. The majority, even those with many victories to their credit, have been mere extensions of their cars, albeit highly skilled and courageous.

MULTI-MILLION POUND INDUSTRY

Grand Prix racing today is certainly a far cry from the early days of the sport. When the Automobile club of France organised the first Grand Prix, in 1906, its members could hardly have imagined how, almost seventy-five years later, the sport would develop into a multi-million pound industry which produces vehicles capable of reaching speeds of almost 200 m.p.h.

Now wide tyres and "skirts," which help create a vacuum under the car, combine to give the car greater adhesion to the track, and so help push up the speeds. Racing on roads, with the exception of the GP's at Monaco and Long Beach, is almost a thing of the past, yet even the man-made circuits are having their safety limits stretched to the fullest by these powerful machines.

Yesterday's heroes would surely survey today's racing scene with amazement — if not approval! Their wheel-to-wheel battles have been replaced by races which have become endurance tests . . . and there's no doubting which the fans would prefer to see. The legendary tussles between Fangio and Moss have no counterpart today, though.

DISTINGUISHED HISTORY

Today, the giants of the sport are the "stables" which produce the cars, the top two, without a doubt, being Ferrari and Lotus.

Since the present form of the World Championship was originated in 1950, these two stables have recorded over 150 GP victories between them, with Ferrari only a nose ahead.

Rival racing teams fall far behind in terms of championship achievement. Several, such as third-placed McLaren, which James Hunt drove to World Championship glory in 1976, have snatched the honours only to find they could not sustain that grade of performance over a longer period of time.

But if life is tough for even the more successful teams, then it's becoming almost impossible for the smaller stables to compete on equal terms. Lord Hesketh discovered that during his brief entry into the sport and private teams like Shadow and Arrows find themselves battling against ever-increasing odds.

However, despite any problem that GP racing may have, despite some unease at the direction in which it sometimes seems to be heading, it does still provide a unique sporting spectacle, with drivers like modern knights mounted on chargers of steel . . . going for glory.

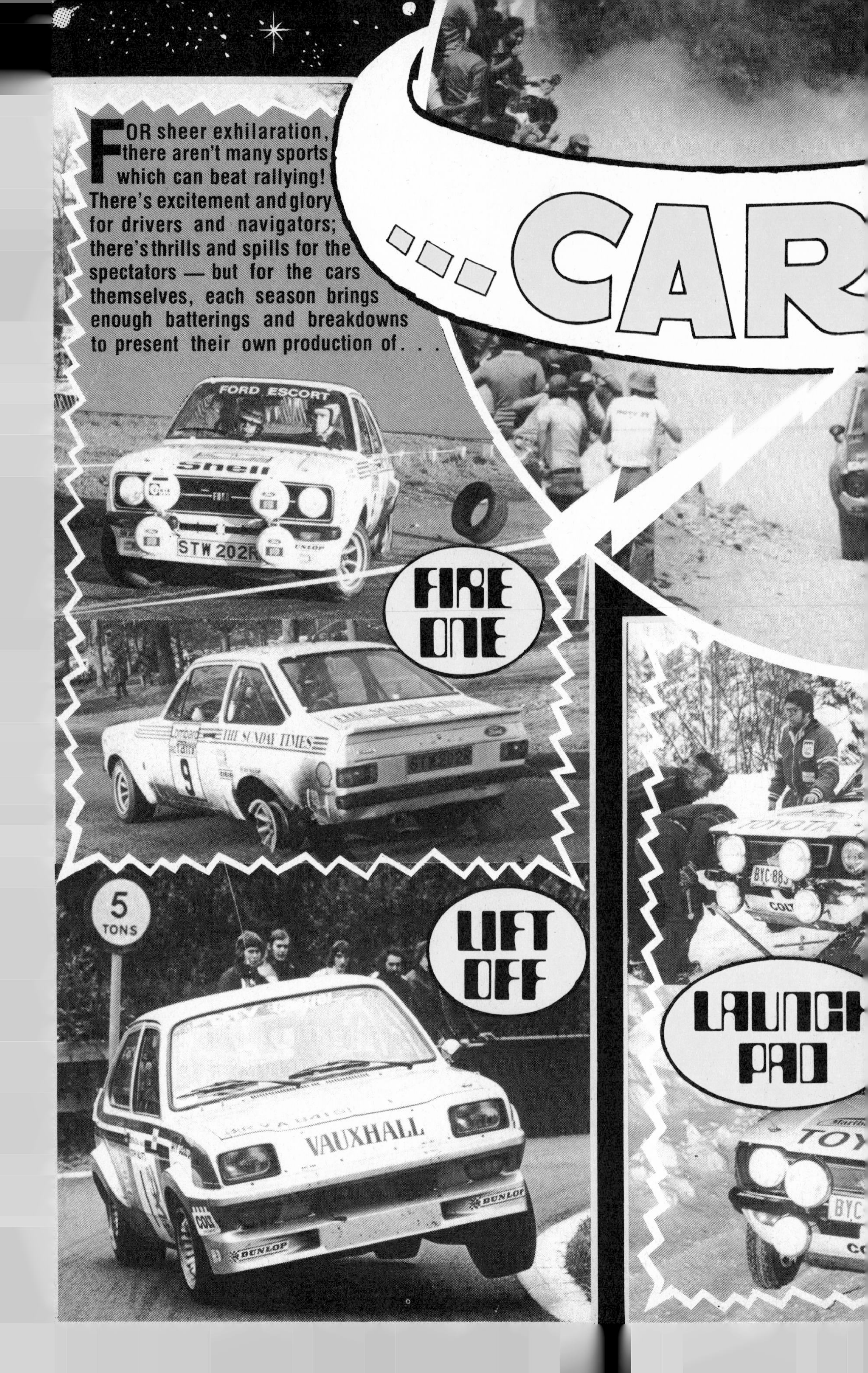
FOR sheer exhilaration, there aren't many sports which can beat rallying! There's excitement and glory for drivers and navigators; there's thrills and spills for the spectators — but for the cars themselves, each season brings enough batterings and breakdowns to present their own production of. . .
...CAR
FORD ESCORT
STW 202R
FIRE ONE
THE SUNDAY TIMES
9
LIFT OFF
5 TONS
VAUXHALL
DUNLOP
TOYOTA
LAUNCH PAD

WARS

BLAST OFF

SOFT LANDING

DEFLECTOR SHIELDS UP

THE 4 SEASONS OF SPORT...

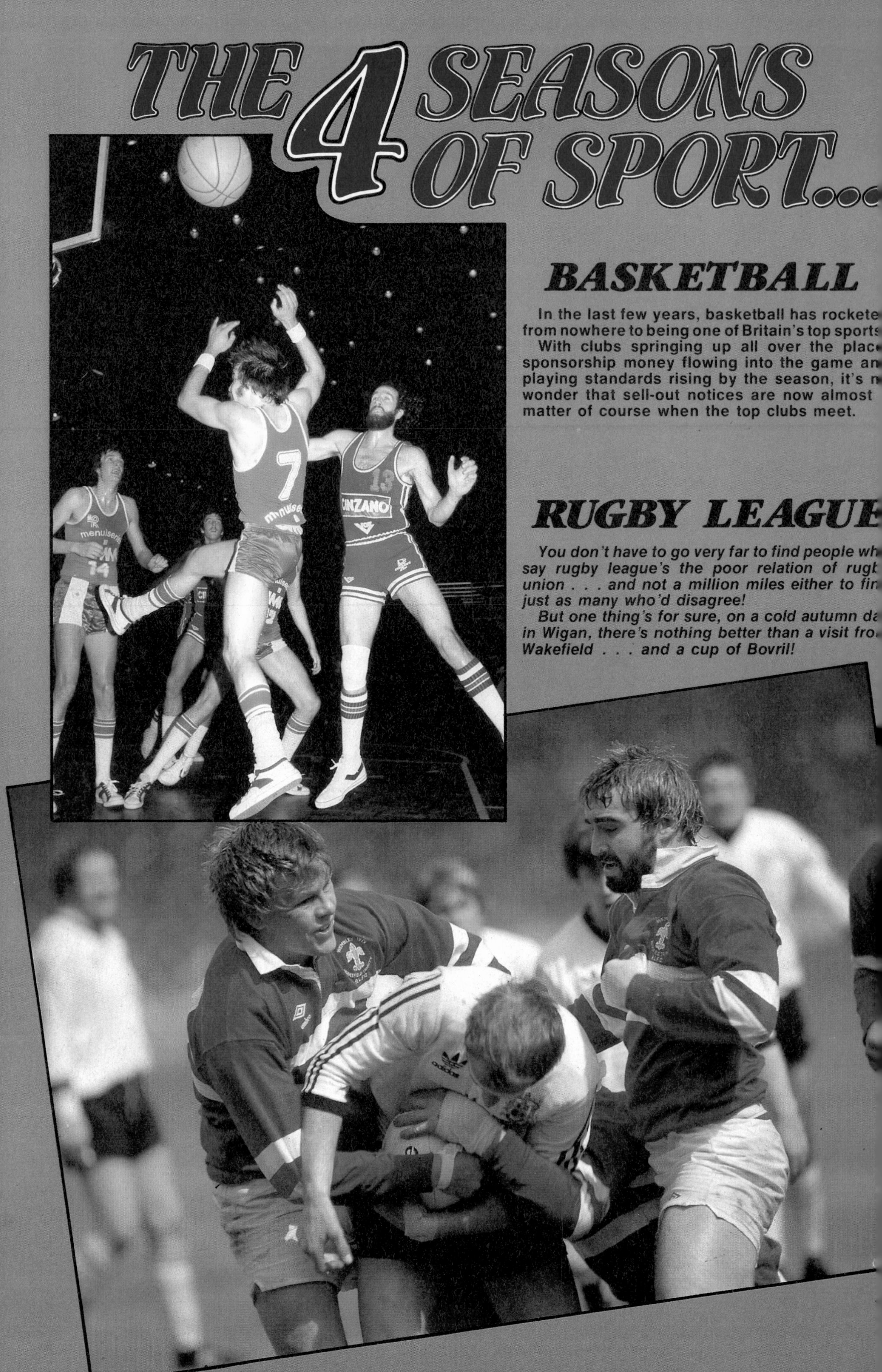

BASKETBALL

In the last few years, basketball has rockete from nowhere to being one of Britain's top sports With clubs springing up all over the plac sponsorship money flowing into the game an playing standards rising by the season, it's n wonder that sell-out notices are now almost matter of course when the top clubs meet.

RUGBY LEAGUE

You don't have to go very far to find people wh say rugby league's the poor relation of rugb union . . . and not a million miles either to fin just as many who'd disagree!

But one thing's for sure, on a cold autumn da in Wigan, there's nothing better than a visit fro Wakefield . . . and a cup of Bovril!

AUTUMN

STAR FOCUS

ILLY BEAUMONT

WITH the looks of a bulldog and something of the physical resence to match, England rugby nion star Billy Beaumont could never e called pin-up material . . . except, f course, amongst those who know a ning or two about rugby.

Ever since his debut for the England ide in New Zealand in 1977, Billy's roved he's a bit special . . . a tremendous scrummager and superb in e loose.

His displays in the second row rought the reward they deserve when e replaced Roger Uttley as captain gainst Ireland in 1979.

Since then the big man's gone on om strength to strength. Salute Billy eaumont — a bulldog with bite!

BADMINTON

With the summer out of the way, badminton clubs all over the country will be getting into action again in super sports complexes and draughty church halls.

But there's another side to badminton — the men who have made it to the top of the international tree, like these two seasoned campaigners Mike Tredgett and Ray Stevens.

BALLBOY
I'M NIPPING DOWN TO MUDCHESTER'S TRAINING GROUND TO ASK THE PLAYERS FOR THEIR AUTOGRAPHS, DAD.

Soon . . .
OOPS! WILL YOU FETCH OUR BALL, SON?
SURE! I'LL KICK IT BACK!

But, on the other side . . .
RIGHT, SOLDIER! TIME TO FIRE OUR COLONEL'S BIRTHDAY SALUTE!

HMM! WONDER WHERE THAT BALL'S GONE?
FIRE!

DUCK
WOW!
BOOM!

CRUMP!
DUCK
DUCK
DUCK
DUCK
GOSH!

TERRIFIC! GREAT SHOT, SON!
YEAH! TREMENDOUS!
FANTASTIC!
PARDON?

Later . . .
. . . SO I DIDN'T GET ANY AUTOGRAPHS, DAD! THE PLAYERS WERE TOO BUSY ASKING FOR MINE. THEY THINK I'M THE GREATEST CANNONBALL SHOT EVER!
?

ALEX "Hurricane" HIGGINS

EDDIE CHARLTON

DENNIS TAYLOR

ON CUE

It's only in recent years that snooker has become "respectable," but thanks to TV and the superb skills of the sport's star players, shown on this page, the game is now booming. Constant practice added to natural ability and intense concentration, has taken these professionals to the very top, so that their play is now delighting millions.

TERRY GRIFFITHS

RAY REARDON

JOHN SPENCER

SCOOP
KEVIN KEEGAN
GREAT
BRITAIN
XI
Admiral

SCOOP
GREAT BRITAIN XI
DANNY McGRAIN

BUSTER
Mal Bagley, known as Buster, is making a name for himself in tennis – both as a player and a hard case.
COP THAT, MATEY!
Now try that one, chum!
Mal's play is being closely studied . . .
Haw, haw! Good job the net was there, or you'd be in the crowd by now!
OOF!
The way Bagley's playing, we just have to pick him, Colonel.
Hrmph! Tennis is supposed to be a game for gentlemen. That roughneck would let the side down.
Finally –
Game, set and match to Bagley!
YIPPEE!

Mal's coach, Clive Neville, meets him as he comes off court . . .
Mal, the Davis Cup selectors want to see you. This could be good news — but watch what you're saying to Colonel Kingsley. He's one of the old brigade.
Meaning he don't like yobs like me? Okay, Clive, if he's nice to me, I'll be nice to him!
Come in, Bagley. Pay close attention to what we have to say.
Blimey! Maybe I should stand to attention and salute!
You're being considered as a member of the British Davis Cup team to play America. Frankly, I'm against it, but a majority of the selectors favour you. I want from you a promise of good behaviour while you're representing your country.
You get no promise from me, Colonel. I'm a professional tennis player, not a crook out on probation! You've seen the way I play — accept me as I am, or forget it!
Impudent young upstart! We're well rid of him!
I'd like to play for my country — but toffee-nosed twits like you get right up my nose.
The Press soon get hold of the story . . .
Hey, Buster, we hear you've turned down a chance to represent your country!
You got it wrong, mate! My country's turned ME down!
Then, on the car radio . . .
Colonel Kingsley, a senior member of the Davis Cup selection committee, has resigned. It is believed there was an argument over the choice of Buster Bagley, who is now confirmed as a member of the team.
Huh! Nobody asked me if I wanted to play! I have to hear the news on the radio!
Stop moaning, Mal. It doesn't fool me! You're dead chuffed!
A fortnight later, Mal joins the rest of the team to fly to America . . .
I'm Simon Tuttle, the non-playing captain in charge. You've already stirred things up, so don't cause any more trouble, Bagley.
You sound like a Colonel Kingsley in the making. What are you, a lance-corporal?

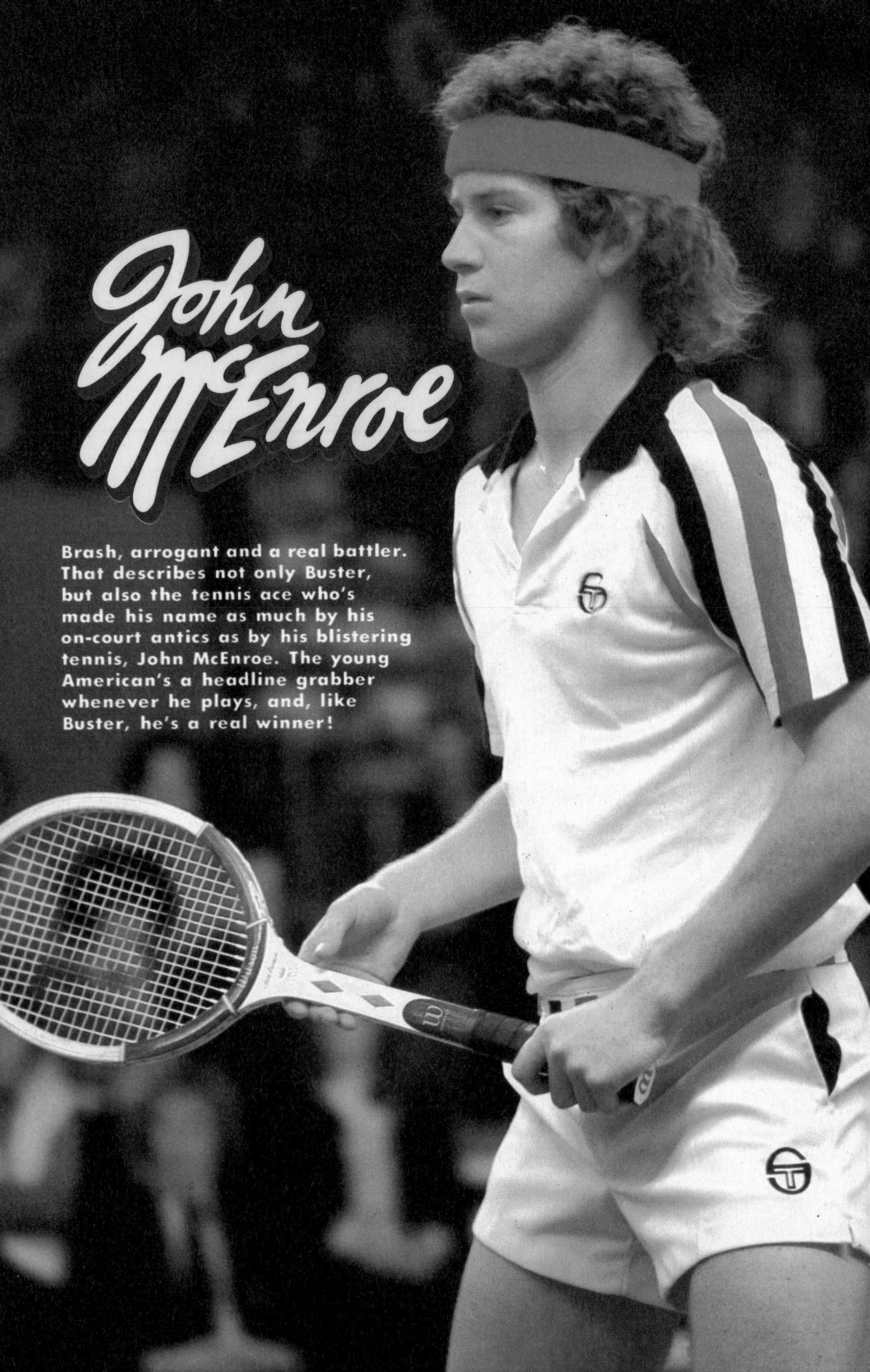
John McEnroe
Brash, arrogant and a real battler.
That describes not only Buster,
but also the tennis ace who's
made his name as much by his
on-court antics as by his blistering
tennis, John McEnroe. The young
American's a headline grabber
whenever he plays, and, like
Buster, he's a real winner!

When the team reaches America . . .
Bagley, smarten yourself up!
I thought we were here to play tennis, not to model clothes.
Never mind the rest, guys — THERE'S Bagley!
What do you think of Britain's chances in the Davis Cup, Buster?
You don't expect me to say we've come all this way to lose, do you? Well, we ain't! We're gonna win!
Mal's first singles match opens the tournament.
You talk big, Bagley. Maybe you're about to eat your words.
We'll soon find out, chum.
How's that for starters?
Harvey's a big hitter, but I can handle him.
Tuttle watches with the British Ambassador, Sir George Webster . . .
First set to Mal. You've got a real find in him, Tuttle.
He put a lot into winning that set. I hope he doesn't fade, Sir George.
Harvey seems to have pulled a muscle – he's limping now. Well, that's his tough luck!
Harvey is obviously hurt. But Bagley is still piling on the pressure. Most unsporting!
Harvey has two choices — to withdraw, or play on. You don't expect Mal to let him win out of sympathy, do you?
Before long –
Game, set and match to Mr Bagley!
MR Bagley! Real polite, these American umpires!

My accident was a bit of luck for you, Bagley.
I'd have beaten you anyway, mate. It just happened quicker.
After Bagley's unsporting behaviour, the crowd are applauding him! Incredible!
Americans play to win, and so does Mal. They appreciate that.
But the British team begin to struggle –
He's lobbed me! I just can't get to grips with this Texan at all.
Never mind, Tony. It just wasn't your day. You'd have beaten him normally.
Only Buster saves the day . . .
Second set to Mr Bagley.
Bagley may be a tough egg – but he certainly can play tennis.
Later, in the team hotel . . .
The doubles will decide the match, but we have a problem. You all told me you didn't wish to be paired with Bagley.
Er — if it helps the team to win, I'll partner him, Simon.
I don't mind pairing with him.
A rush of volunteers! You don't like me, but you like the way I play. I'll take Roger Quayle. He went down fighting in the singles, and I reckon we can make a team.
I make the decisions, Bagley. But, er, I agree to your suggestion.
You ain't got no choice if you want to win. Come on, Quayle, we'll get some practice together.
The final match . . .
Well, this is it. We're 2-2 in the contest, so we have to win this one to lift the cup. Remember what we worked out in practice.
I'm not a beginner, Bagley.
AN ACE! That's got us off to a good start!

But as the match progresses . . .
Wake up, partner! You could have got that one!
Here comes another one that Quayle ain't going to try for.
OUT OF MY WAY!
URGH!
That's how it's done, Quayle! Get the idea?
What do you think you're playing at, Bagley?
Tennis, mate! And if you're just here to make up the numbers, I'll beat them two on me own!
I'll show you, big mouth!
That's livened him up!
Now he's settled down, Roger is playing a storming game.
Nearly as good as Bagley's! But it needed Mal to get him going!

Nice one, partner! Now we're really getting to them!
MINE!
And mine again! We've done it, partner!
Game, set and match to Mr Bagley and Mr Quayle!
After the presentation—
Come and be photographed with the cup, chaps. Where's Bagley?
That scruff would only spoil the pictures, anyway.
Strewth! There he is over there — swamped by newsmen!
You won the cup practically single-handed, Buster — you were better than the rest of your team put together!
You've gone down real big over here, Buster. I run a country club and tennis school in Florida. I want you as my chief coach. Name your own fee!
What! Bagley's being offered a fortune to stay in the States!
PHEW!
But no thanks, mister. I ain't ready to teach yet. I've got a lot to learn still, and the way to do that is to keep playing in tough tournaments. I'm going home with the rest of the team. Think how they'd miss me!
The End

SECOND-HALF OF COMPUTER SOCCER (CONTINUED FROM PAGE 58)

INTERNATIONAL COMPUTER SOCCER

GREAT BRITAIN v. THE REST OF THE WORLD

PENALTY DECIDER!

The Rest of the World give the homesters a fright straight from the restart. A left-foot shot by Platini from the corner of the penalty box flashes just past the post.

The World force two corners in quick succession immediately after this, but no goals come from either.

Maradona does well to dispossess Sansom, but Rummenigge hits the ball well over from 25 yards following the Argentinian's lay-back.

The opening stages of the second half have shown that the World have shaken themselves up and are taking the game to the Great Britain team.

The visitors are only inches away from taking the lead in 52 minutes. An inswinging Dirceu corner causes all sorts of trouble. Shilton, challenged by Krankl, can only punch the ball straight up in the air. When Kempes leaps to head down at the near post, McGrain clears off the line.

KEVIN KEEGAN – GOALSCORER FOR GREAT BRITAIN

A minute later Kaltz comes close with a 30-yard drive.

Great Britain come to life when Dalglish feeds Keegan who crashes the ball against the side net. Maradona resumes the World attack when he crosses from the right but Rummenigge can't control the ball on the edge of the six-yard box and Shilton grabs the loose ball.

In 57 minutes Keegan intercepts a Robertson cross which seems bound for Hellstrom. His lob shot drifts harmlessly over the bar, however.

Kempes nutmegs McQueen and shoots from 20 yards. Shilton has to scramble to dive and parry the ball.

PENALTY CLAIM

In sixty minutes there are penalty claims from the World team when Sansom handles on the edge of the box.

The referee rules that the offence took place outside.

Cabrini's free-kick is punched clear from the head of Pezzey by Shilton.

Shilton comes to Britain's rescue again two minutes later, when a World move rips his defence apart. Maradona runs to the by-line and cuts back to Krankl who flicks on to Kempes.

Kempes' shot is magnificently parried by Shilton, when the ball rebounds to Kempes he shoots past.

The British 'keeper is called into action again four minutes later but this time he gives away a penalty.

A powerful run by Tresor takes him deep into the British penalty box but wide of the goal. He looks a certainty to cut the ball back to Krankl who's in the clear but Shilton runs off his line to meet him. Tresor rounds him but is brought down by the 'keeper. The referee has no hesitation in pointing to the spot.

DIRCEU makes no mistake with the kick.

GREAT BRITAIN 1 REST OF THE WORLD 2

Britain reply right away with a Brooking shot from 18 yards.

At the other end Kempes sprints past McGrain to reach the by-line, but his cross is blasted past by Platini.

Britain are now very disjointed and have lost much of their composure up front.

In 64 minutes, McGrain is unlucky when, after a good move, the ball takes a bad bounce and his mishit shot screws wide.

At the other end Krankl misses an easy chance when he miskicks a cross in front of goal.

PRESSURE

Britain force a corner on the right. McQueen jumps high above Pezzey but his header skims the top of the cross-bar. Hoddle hammers a shot well wide as Britain at last mount some pressure.

Britain are awarded a free-kick out on the right touch line. Wilkins floats the ball over and Hellstrom is challenged by Dalglish. The big Swede drops the ball and it is going over the line. Cabrini, seeing the danger, leaps forward and in dramatic fashion overhead-kicks the ball off the line to prevent the equaliser.

PLEASE SHOW ACTION REPLAY OF CABRINI'S SPECTACULAR GOAL-LINE CLEARANCE.

HELLSTROM LOOKS ON HELPLESSLY AS CABRINI LAUNCHES HIMSELF AT THE BALL.

The World's reply is a through ball from Kaltz to Maradona. The little Argentinian is thwarted by Shilton who runs outside his box to thump the ball clear.

In 72 minutes a Platini free-kick is headed over by Rummenigge.

In 75 minutes Burns brilliantly intercepts a Kaltz pass as Krankl and Kempes are queueing up to score.

Dalglish gets free from Pezzey for once and manages a shot at goal, but Hellstrom saves easily. In 80 minutes Great Britain make their best chance of the half and miss it.

Keegan slips a great ball to Brooking in the box. He drives at goal but Hellstrom dives to turn the ball round the post for a corner.

Pezzey heads the corner kick clear but Hellstrom has to clutch safely to hold a Wilkins first-time lob from twenty

In these last minutes Britain are having their best spell of the second half, as they go all out for the equaliser.

DIEGO MARADONA – A WORLD-CLASS PLAYER

As the referee checks his watch Dalglish intercepts a poor Cabrini pass and lets loose a piledriver from thirty yards. The ball beats Hellstrom but cannons off the post and goes out of play.

FULL-TIME: GREAT BRITAIN XI 1
THE REST OF THE WORLD 2

COMPUTER ANALYSIS OF MATCH

After dominating the first half, the G.B. side paid for not taking their chances. The Rest of the World raised their game in the second half and gladly accepted the penalty award. A draw possibly would have been a fair result on the ninety minutes' play.

MERIT STARS

GREAT BRITAIN

SHILTON ★★★★
McGRAIN ★★★★★
BURNS ★★★★
McQUEEN ★★★
SANSOM ★★★
HODDLE ★★★
WILKINS ★★★★
BROOKING ★★★
KEEGAN ★★★★
DALGLISH ★★★
ROBERTSON ★★★

REST OF THE WORLD

HELLSTROM ★★★★★
KALTZ ★★★
PEZZEY ★★★★
TRESOR ★★★
CABRINI ★★★
MARADONA ★★★★★
RUMMENIGGE ★★★
PLATINI ★★★
DIRCEU ★★★
KRANKL ★★★
KEMPES ★★★★

MAUGER THE MIGHTY

★ STAR FOCUS

IVAN first arrived in this country from his native New Zealand in the Fifties and during the Sixties he established himself as a fast-gating rider of tremendous potential — which wasn't long in being fully developed.

He started the Seventies by becoming the first rider to win three consecutive world championships and ended the decade by winning it for a record-breaking sixth time.

In between, Ivan won every honour speedway had to offer at both national and international level, including three World Long Track Championships, two World Best Pairs titles and four World Team Cup trophies, with both Britain and New Zealand and he was rewarded for his services to the sport with the M.B.E..

Never universally popular because of his ultra-professional attitude both on and off the track, Ivan nevertheless has earned the acclaim of being speedway's greatest-ever. And despite now being in his forties and entering his fourth decade of racing, there's no sign of him slowing down in the Eighties!

QUIZTIME!

(ANSWERS ON PAGE 19

MOTOR SPORT

1. Which driver won four Formula 1 Grand Prix races in 1979, yet didn't win the Drivers' Championship?
2. Which British island do you associate with T.T. motor cycle racing?
3. In which country is the Kyalami circuit?
4. What nationality is rally driver Timo Makinen?
5. How many times in the Seventies did Peter Collins win the World Individual Speedway Championship?
6. With which motor sport is Johnny Cecotto associated?

GOLF

1. Which of these golf courses is the odd one out? — Gleneagles, Turnberry, St Andrews, Muirfield and Carnoustie.
2. Where was the British Open held in 1980?
3. How many "woods" is a golfer allowed to carry in his golf bag?
4. From which countries do the following golfers come from? — DALE HAYES, GREG NORMAN, MICHAEL KING and SAM TORRANCE?
5. The famous U.S. Masters golf tournament was founded by a group of American teachers. True or false?
6. Where is the "home" of the Royal and Ancient Golf Club?

ATHLETICS

1. Which piece of equipment is being described here? "Made of soli iron, brass or any metal not softer than brass, or a filled shell c such metal, it must be spherical and smooth surfaced. Th minimum weight for men is 16 pounds."
2. In 1979, Sebastian Coe broke three world records in two month over distances of 800 m, 1500 m and 1 mile. But in which orde did he break them?
3. After a false start in track events, how are the runners recalled
4. The 1948 Olympic Games were held in London. True or False?
5. The 1968 Olympic Games will always be especially remembere for two athletes — a long jumper who astounded the world and high jumper who created a new style. Who were they?
6. What connection is there between top British runners Paula Fudg and Ann Ford?

BOXING

1. What do the following abbreviations stand for? A.B.A.: E.B.U. W.B.C.?
2. Boxers called Joe Dundee, Johnny Dundee and Vince Dundee a held world titles, yet none of them came from Scotland. True o False?
3. A boxer, later to become a world-famous professional, won th Olympic Light-Heavyweight gold medal at Rome in 1960. Who wa he?
4. Only one British boxer ever put Muhammud Ali on the floor. Wh was he?
5. In recent years, Scotland has had two World Lightweigh champions in Ken Buchanan and Jim Watt. But have they eve fought each other?
6. At which weight does John Conteh fight?

OOTBALL

Think back to the last World Cup Final. What number did Argentina's Osvaldo Ardiles wear against Holland?

Who or what is Sincil Bank?

Which member of the "royal" family has appeared in a Cup Final?

He was born in Skegness, his middle name is the same as the surname of an England team-mate, and his football career started with Scunthorpe. Who is he?

What eight things must a referee carry on to the field with him?

Football was introduced to Scotland by an eighteenth-century saint called St Johnstone. True or false?

For which countries do the following players play? — RONNIE HELLSTROM, PAOLO ROSSI, MARIUS TRESOR and MOHAMMED ALI BEN MOUSSA?

If you were watching a match between Atvidaberg and IFK Gothenburg, which country would you be in?

UGBY

Who are "The Pumas?"

When was rugby league first begun — 1895, 1900, 1926 or 1951?

Who captained Wales in the 1980 Five Nations Championships?

Which rugby ground is famed for its under-soil heating system? TWICKENHAM, NATIONAL STADIUM, CARDIFF, LANSDOWNE ROAD or MURRAYFIELD.

Up until the First World War, rugby was played with a spherical ball. It wasn't until 1919 that an oval ball was introduced. True or false?

A famous Welsh rugby union club plays at a ground with a name which is usually associated with rugby league. The ground is called St Helens — what is the club?

CRICKET

1. Overarm bowling was invented by a woman. True or False?
2. In the tour of Australia last winter, a player became one of England's youngest-ever captains. Who was he?
3. Can a fielder use a cap to field the ball?
4. Which two Championship counties are the farthest apart?
5. The following old-time players are usually associated with one aspect of cricket. For example, Sir Donald Bradman is associated with batting. Can you tell what the following players were famous for? JACK HOBBS, JIM LAKER, LEN HUTTON and WALLY HAMMOND.
6. Which County side plays at the Kennington Oval?

TENNIS

1. Why do the Irish Lawn Tennis Championships hold a unique place in tennis history?
2. Before they married, what were the surnames of Chris Lloyd, Billie Jean King and Evonne Cawley?
3. Wimbledon's Centenary Ladies' Singles Championship was won by Virginia Wade. In which year?
4. Ilie Nastase has never won the Men's Singles at Wimbledon. True or false?
5. Who contested the 1979 Men's Singles Final at Wimbledon?
6. Where does tennis star Victor Pecci come from?

ANSWERS TO PHOTO QUIZ
Pages 18 and 19

1. Yes, drivers may rejoin the race after leaving the track, as long as they don't interfere with any other driver.
2. C and I .
3. Glenn Hoddle, Justin Fashanu (left) and Kevin Bond (right).
4. Tennis stars Sue Barker and John McEnroe.
5. No, amateur bouts are allowed with only two ropes.
6. Osvaldo Ardiles, River Plate Stadium, Buenos Aires, Argentina. Kenny Burns, Hampden Park, Glasgow, Scotland.
7. Wayne Player.
8. The umpire would give "not out" because the wicket keeper must be wholly behind the stumps until the ball has made contact with, or passed the bat.

WHEN it comes to Association Football, the Australians are pretty good cricketers. Their best team can occasionally — purely by luck, of course, out-play ours, and even their touring rugby sides turn out more-than-workman-like performances.

At tennis they have produced more than their fair share of champions and their swimmers have been hoarding world records like stamps for years. But at football —they aren't all that hot and when the odds were drawn up for teams competing in the 1990 World Cup in Russia, you could get 600-1 against Australia.

They weren't even expected to qualify until they were lucky enough to be drawn in a group with Formosa and a group of tiny Pacific islands called the New Hebrides.

The Aussies beat Formosa in Sydney and then drew 2-2 away from home.

The average age of the New Hebridean side was 13 years 8 months. Even so, the Australians only scraped home by a single goal margin both away and at home. Nevertheless, they qualified for Russia and flew out with high aims and low hopes. It would have been no hopes at all, but for their secret weapon!

All the players were "secret" — none of the teams competing in the Cup proper had bothered to send scouts to the qualifying matches — but one player was more of a secret than the others. He hadn't even played in the qualifying games and the few times he had trained with the team, it had been behind locked doors and with the strictest of security precautions.

His name was Kenny Young and although he was a registered player, he was unconnected with any of the Australian League sides.

He was a Mystery Man with capital Ms.

When the team were photographed leaving the plane at Moscow Airport part of the mystery was cleared up. They at least knew who Kenny Young was. He was an aborigine with a grin like a crescent moon and a sing-song voice. But his skill as a footballer remained unknown until the first match in the Australian's sub-group.

SHOCKS GALORE

THE section included an African country, Pohlia, who were the favourite Dark Continent side to reach the finals proper, and little-known Arab state from the Petrol Gulf, Abu Dahban.

The Aussies' first match was against

KENNY the KANGAROO

SCOOP Tall Tale No. 2

.bu Dahban. The Arabs had been trained t ludicrous expense by Europe's finest :oaches and as players they were as good s they could be taught to be. Many of the 0,000 spectators in the stadium fancied hem to beat the Aussies with lots to spare nd no-one even noticed that Kenny 'oung, the Mystery Man, trotted out vearing the Australian No. 9 shirt. None of heir forward line were famous names nyway.

Abu Dahban showed their drilled skill traight from the kick-off. They immediately fell into a rigid and orthodox -2-4 pattern. The centre-forward flicked he ball to the inside-left, who passed back o the inside-right, who was playing in midfield role.

The forwards moved towards the Australian goal just as they had been instructed to, and accurate, stabbed passes ierced the defence sufficiently for the entre-forward to get in his shot. It had ower and direction but lacked the magic hat gives goal-grabbers goals. The ustralian goalie dropped to his knees nd managed to scramble the ball round he post.

The same mixture of skill and scramble vas evident when the corner kick was ver. The Abu Dahban inside-left got a oot to it, and the Australian right-back idn't quite manage to get his head out of ts way. The ball ricocheted upfield, the ttack was broken up, and the full-back ad a headache for a week.

There followed a long patch of muddled lay in the midfield. Each time the Abu Dahban forwards began to build up an ttack, an Australian would stick a head or foot or a knee in the way of a vital pass nd, more by luck than judgment, break t up.

It was from the Australian right-half's ibs that the ball finally bounced to Kenny 'oung. He trapped it neatly and then egan to move purposefully upfield.

The Abu Dahban defence, swinging into ction for the first time, remembered what he text-books and trainers had said about lealing with a lone attack and moved ccordingly.

What happened next amazed the crowds, stunned the sports-writers and bsolutely flabbergasted the Abu Dahban lefence. As their centre-half moved into he tackle, Kenny Young slid the ball past im. Then, without breaking his stride, he eapt!

He was ten years too late. In 1980 he'd ave won an Olympic gold medal — for he high jump! His leap carried him leanly and effortlessly over the centre-alf's head — and landed him within inches of the still-moving ball. The Abu Dahban full-backs looked as if they'd been pole-axed. They just stood, mouths agape, as Kenny the Kangaroo bounded by and snapped the ball into the net for the first goal of the match. It was fully thirty seconds before the crowd recovered themselves enough to cheer — then they almost lifted the roof off the stands.

Kenny Young had been born in the outback, the Australian bush. All his life kangaroos had been his companions and playmates — and he certainly learnt a lot from them. The muscles of his legs were tremendously developed and they could send him soaring through the air with the minimum of effort.

By half-time, Australia — or more accurately, Kenny the Kangaroo — had built up a three-goal lead.

His second goal had come from a corner — no-one stood a snowflake on a stove's chance of beating the Kangaroo in the air, and he completed his hat-trick by lobbing the ball over the Arab goalie's head as he advanced — and then lobbing himself after it!

The pattern was repeated in the second half. Australia beat Abu Dahban by five goals, all of them scored by Kenny Young!

Telex wires all over the world were set humming and the incredible leaping Australian was on his way into the headlines and the history books.

The spectators who poured out of the stadium that day were all talking excitedly, hands waving, heads shaking, about the aborigine with the phenomenal leap. All the spectators bar one, that is, a man whose dark face was darker than usual. He was Odinga Nkoma, manager and scout for the Pohlian national team!

STOP KENNY YOUNG!

ODINGA NKOMA had difficulty in getting to sleep that night and when he tried counting sheep they changed quickly into the form of a grinning aborigine in a number 9 shirt soaring high on his way to score more goals.

A player like Kenny Young could have given even a defence as strong as England's or as numerous as Italy's a lot of problems and Pohlia's defence wasn't really above good First Division standard. There was only one chance and Odinga Nkoma had it in his team!

The man in question was Nogobo Ngoobo and he was the Pohlia team's third-choice goalkeeper. He wasn't much of a goalkeeper but he was seven feet eleven inches tall! Odinga Nkoma decided to convert Nogobo from a goal-keeper to a centre-half! His reasoning being that if anyone could stop Kenny it would be the giant — and if he couldn't, well, no-one else could!

When Kenny Young saw the opposing centre-half, he turned grey. He wasn't at all sure he could leap over eight feet of muscle and bone without a pole to vault with!

The game began and the Pohlians almost fed the ball to Kenny, so anxious were they to see how he would fare!

Kenny picked up a loose pass, gulped and set off upfield. The forward line let him through. The right-half let him through. The left-half let him through. Nogobo Ngoobo moved purposefully and massively into his path, backed by his two full-backs.

Kenny slid the ball past the giant's outstretched foot, bunched his muscular legs and bounded towards the grey Russian sky.

One hundred thousand hands covered one hundred thousand eyes. But the spectators still heard the sickening thud — for Kenny the Kangaroo hadn't made it.

When the spectators peeked through their spread fingers they saw both players lying motionless on the ground. Stretchers were brought on. Kenny was carried off. Nogobo Ngoobo wouldn't fit and in the end, two stretchers had to be tied together to bear his huge frame from the field.

With substitutes, the match re-started. It was a scrappy game but Pohlia ran out lucky winners by a scrambled goal in the last minute. They eventually went on to qualify by heading their section.

And Kenny the Kangaroo? He was fit in time to watch the finals — from the stands.

Then he flew back to Australia with his team-mates and went back to the bush of the outback and his friends the kangaroos.

So, as we approach the 1982 World Cup in Spain, it might not do any harm if football team managers included an eight-foot giant in their World Cup plans — just in case!!

THIS GOALIE'S GOT GUTS!
Ben Leiper, doctor and goalkeeper combined, takes a break from Mancastor City's tough league programme to play for England. Now with only seconds to go and England leading Bulgaria 1-0, Ben has to face a vital penalty . . .
Ben's saved it. HE'S WON THE MATCH FOR ENGLAND!
The fans are right, England run off as winners. Next day at the hospital . . .
Congratulations, Ben. That was some match last night. Must've been one of your toughest ever!
Well, no. Actually the toughest game I remember was when City were struggling to get out of the Fourth Division . . . if you lot put me down, I'll tell you about it . . .
CITY! CITY!
"The club was broke, our playing strength down to twelve men . . ."
You couldn't call this text book training, lads, but it's good exercise — and we can't afford groundsmen. Haul away!
BRITISH
I've always wanted to be Ben Hur. Gid up, serfs.
AAH!
THE CLOWN'S FALLEN!
Get me a sling, Ernie. Looks as if Tony's broken his collarbone.
LTD
Stone me! That means we don't even have a sub. for Saturday's match, and against Slagley Rovers we'll need one — they're real tough nuts!

"Saturday . . ."
You've got to win today, Ben, to stay in the promotion race, and between you and me if we can't make it up this year the club's finished! The bankers are starting to make nasty noises!
We'll be doing our best, Ernie — it's all we can do!
"The ref set the game in motion . . ."
Slagley are bashing their way through right from the kick-off.
No sweat. They'll have to finish better than that. Doesn't look as if he's going to stop at hitting the ball though!
Goin' somewhere, mate?
UUR!
Slagley have pushed too many men forward. Break quickly, Dave!
Nobody makes a fool of me, mate. I'LL GET YOU NEXT TIME!
WE WERE THROUGH THERE! BUT THEY'VE CHOPPED JIMMY WORTH DOWN!
UNGH!

Hey, how about a foul, ref?
I keep the game moving. That's what the fans want. Play on!
"Slagley were giving me the works!"
OUCH! GET YOUR ELBOWS OUT OF MY RIBS, YOU BIG APES!
Ben's down! But the ref's letting it go!
WAKEN UP, REF! THIS ISN'T A RE-RUN OF THE SECOND WORLD WAR, YOU KNOW!
OOF!
Are you okay, Ben?
What's a bruise more or less? I'll take the free kick. Get the lads well upfield.
Wow! What a kick! Nearly end to end!
Ben's got us away!
"Jimmy Worth makes no mistake . . ."
GOAL!

Gosh, the Slagley fans are worse than their players! We'll be lucky to get out of this match in one piece!
RUBBISH, REF!
That keeper, Leiper, is the one holdin' City together!
Don't worry, we'll get the ball in his net — and him as well, if necessary.
Missed again, chum.
ANDREWS
SHIFT IT, LADS.
"Next moment, I was chopped down – behind the ref's back!"
COP THAT, MATE!
AAH!
"They really gave me a pasting!"
MY HANDS!

I can't use my hands properly! They duffed me up deliberately. And the ref didn't see a thing.
Let's see 'im performin' heroics now!
"The next attack, and I was in real trouble!"
OUCH! I CAN'T HOLD IT!
TETLEY
"Five minutes later, the inevitable happened . . ."
Blimey! Ben's heading the ball instead of handling it!
They've equalised! And I couldn't do a thing to stop it!
"Half-time . . ."
You'd better go in goal, Andy. I'll play in the outfield. I can't come off, or we'll be down to ten men.
If we can beat this lot, we'll DESERVE promotion!
Hey, the mugs have got their 'keeper playin' outfield. WE'LL MURDER 'EM NOW!
I let that goal in, so it's up to me to make up for it.
URGH! CLOGGED AGAIN. BUT THE REF'S BLOWING THIS TIME!

SCOOP
GREAT BRITAIN XI
PETER SHILTON

"I took the kick myself."
Spot, on Ben.
BLAST, HE'S SAVED IT!
"Jimmy Worth reached my corner brilliantly, but . . ."
HOPKI
The 'keeper's reached it again. He's some player!
That's a poor throw by the 'keeper though. Maybe I can reach it.
HEY, REF. GIVE US A CHANCE TO PLAY FOOTBALL.
Urr! He's hit me in the face! And the ref isn't blowing!

BLIMEY!
I've had enough of you lot trying to kick me off the park! **GIMME THE BALL!**

LET'S HAVE ONE, BEN!

PENALTY, REF!
AAH!

Nobody wants to take the penalty, Ben. How about you?
Crikey! Okay, I'll have a go, boys.

IT'S THERE! YAHOO!

"We won 2-1 and that was really how our climb to the top began."

You played a blinder there, Ben.

Thanks, chum. Ouch, watch the mitt! I reckon I ought to see a doctor!

AND AS YOU ALL KNOW, CITY CERTAINLY DID!

Ole Olsen
Carlsberg
EYFRIARS

SPEEDWAY
FOCUS ON SPEED

Although similar forms of the sport existed in America and South Africa, it was really in 1923 in Maitland, Australia — at, of all things, an agricultural show — that speedway really began. Its popularity spread rapidly, and the sport has since extended its international boundaries from the Eastern European nations to Scandinavia to outposts in Israel and the Middle East and, of course, to these shores, where it now lays claim to being the country's second most-popular spectator sport.

With almost 40 tracks in operation every week, the sport enjoyed a boom period during the 1970s — though it couldn't hope to match the attendances of the Thirties and Forties, where "Full House" notices regularly appeared outside stadia, with 50,000 fans packed inside. In these days, top riders could earn as much in one night's racing as today's soccer stars earn in a month!

PROFESSIONALISM

In recent times, one rider more than any other has brought an air of professionalism to speedway. Six-times world champion Ivan Mauger — awarded an M.B.E. for his efforts — has not only been the top individual performer of the last decade but he has made his influence felt throughout the sport. From first guiding Britain to World Team Cup success, to leading his native New Zealand to their first-ever victory in that championship, Ivan has led the way.

Triple world champion Ole Olsen, a one-time Mauger protege, owes much to the "old master" and in turn the Great Dane has revitalised speedway in his home country, bringing out the potential of riders of the calibre of Hans Nielsen and Finn Thomsen, and transforming Denmark into Scandinavia's number-one speedway nation, a position long held by Sweden.

Since the retirement of five-times world champion Ove Fundin, Sweden's speedway fortunes have gradually declined, with only Anders Michanek and Jan Andersson showing true international class.

TRADITIONAL RIVALS

One nation whose fortunes are definitely improving, however, is America, which has sprung to the forefront of the international arena since its top riders started drifting over in increasing numbers to race in the British League. Scott Autrey, Bruce Penhall, Kelly Moran, Bobby Schwartz — that's the sort of backbone that any speedway nation would envy.

They would certainly be welcomed by their traditional rivals, Russia, who dominate ice speedway but haven't, since the days of Igor Plechanov and Boris Samorodov, been able to produce top-quality riders on shale. Neighbours Czechoslovakia fare better, with the Verner brothers, Ales Dryml and Zdenek Kudrna — solid Czech-mates at Exeter — prominent, while Polish riders, such as Zenon Plech, are traditionally typified by the sort of skills displayed by their countrymen who were Spitfire pilots in the war — a daredevil sense of bravery!

STRENGTH-IN-DEPTH

The one thing that all these riders have in common is that they race for teams in the British League, the toughest and most competitive in the world. It was the experience of racing against opposition of this calibre on a regular basis that helped England to reign supreme till the latter part of the Seventies. Peter Collins, Malcolm Simmons, Dave Jessup, Gordon Kennett, John Davis and John Louis all contributed to 3 World Team Cup and 3 World Best Pairs Championships, with "P.C." becoming England's first individual World Champion for 18 years.

And the future . . .? Indoor speedway has already arrived to complement the traditional form of the sport, so it seems certain that speedway will continue to prosper — sliding to success!

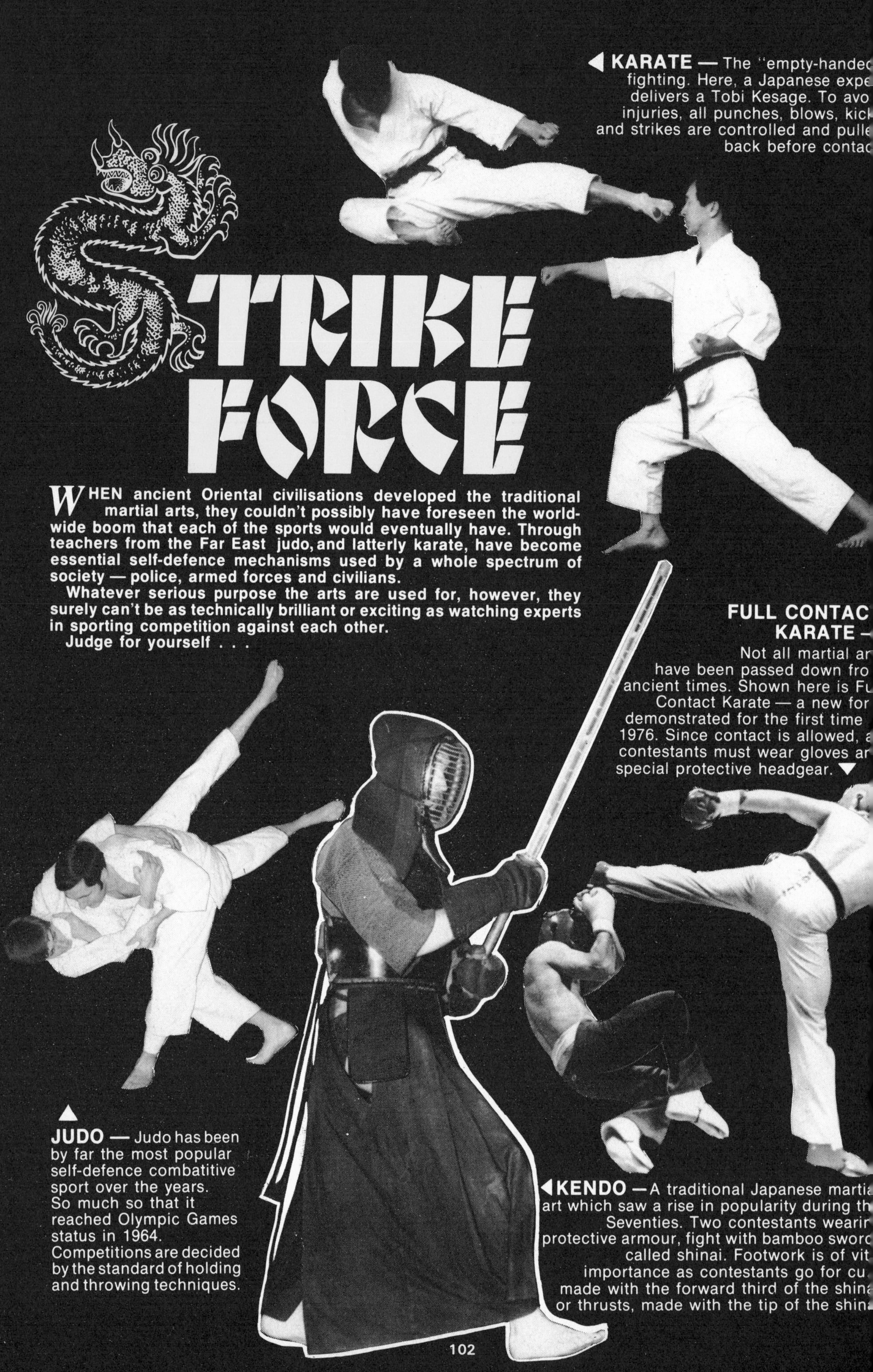

STRIKE FORCE

WHEN ancient Oriental civilisations developed the traditional martial arts, they couldn't possibly have foreseen the world-wide boom that each of the sports would eventually have. Through teachers from the Far East judo, and latterly karate, have become essential self-defence mechanisms used by a whole spectrum of society — police, armed forces and civilians.

Whatever serious purpose the arts are used for, however, they surely can't be as technically brilliant or exciting as watching experts in sporting competition against each other.

Judge for yourself . . .

◀ **KARATE** — The "empty-handed fighting. Here, a Japanese expe delivers a Tobi Kesage. To avo injuries, all punches, blows, kick and strikes are controlled and pulle back before contac

FULL CONTAC KARATE — Not all martial ar have been passed down fro ancient times. Shown here is Fu Contact Karate — a new for demonstrated for the first time 1976. Since contact is allowed, a contestants must wear gloves ar special protective headgear. ▼

▲ **JUDO** — Judo has been by far the most popular self-defence combatitive sport over the years. So much so that it reached Olympic Games status in 1964. Competitions are decided by the standard of holding and throwing techniques.

◀ **KENDO** — A traditional Japanese martia art which saw a rise in popularity during th Seventies. Two contestants wearin protective armour, fight with bamboo sword called shinai. Footwork is of vit importance as contestants go for cu made with the forward third of the shina or thrusts, made with the tip of the shina

KLOG
SCOOP'S
STONE-AGE
SOCCER
STAR
I HATE TIMES LIKE THIS . . .
. . . 0-0. A PENALTY TO US AND ONLY A MINUTE TO GO.
IF I SCORE, WE WIN THE LEAGUE. BUT WHAT IF I MISS?
DON'T BE SILLY, KLOG! IT'S ONLY A GAME! IF YOU MISS, YOU MISS!
WINNING ISN'T EVERYTHING! IT'S THE GAME THAT COUNTS—THE SPORTSMANSHIP!
HEH! HEH! YEP! IT'S ONLY A GAME!
WHAT D'YOU THINK YOU'RE DOING? YOU SAVED MY PENALTY!!!
QUAKE! QUIVER! SHUDDER!

SCOOP
KENNY SANSOM
GREAT BRITAIN XI

adidas
SCOOP
GREAT
BRITAIN
XI
KENNY BURNS

'KEEPERS IN CLO

'KEEPERS come in all shapes and sizes and they all have their own individual styles. I've picked these pictures to show how top 'keepers cope with all the different problems that come a goalie's way.
Hope you like 'em.

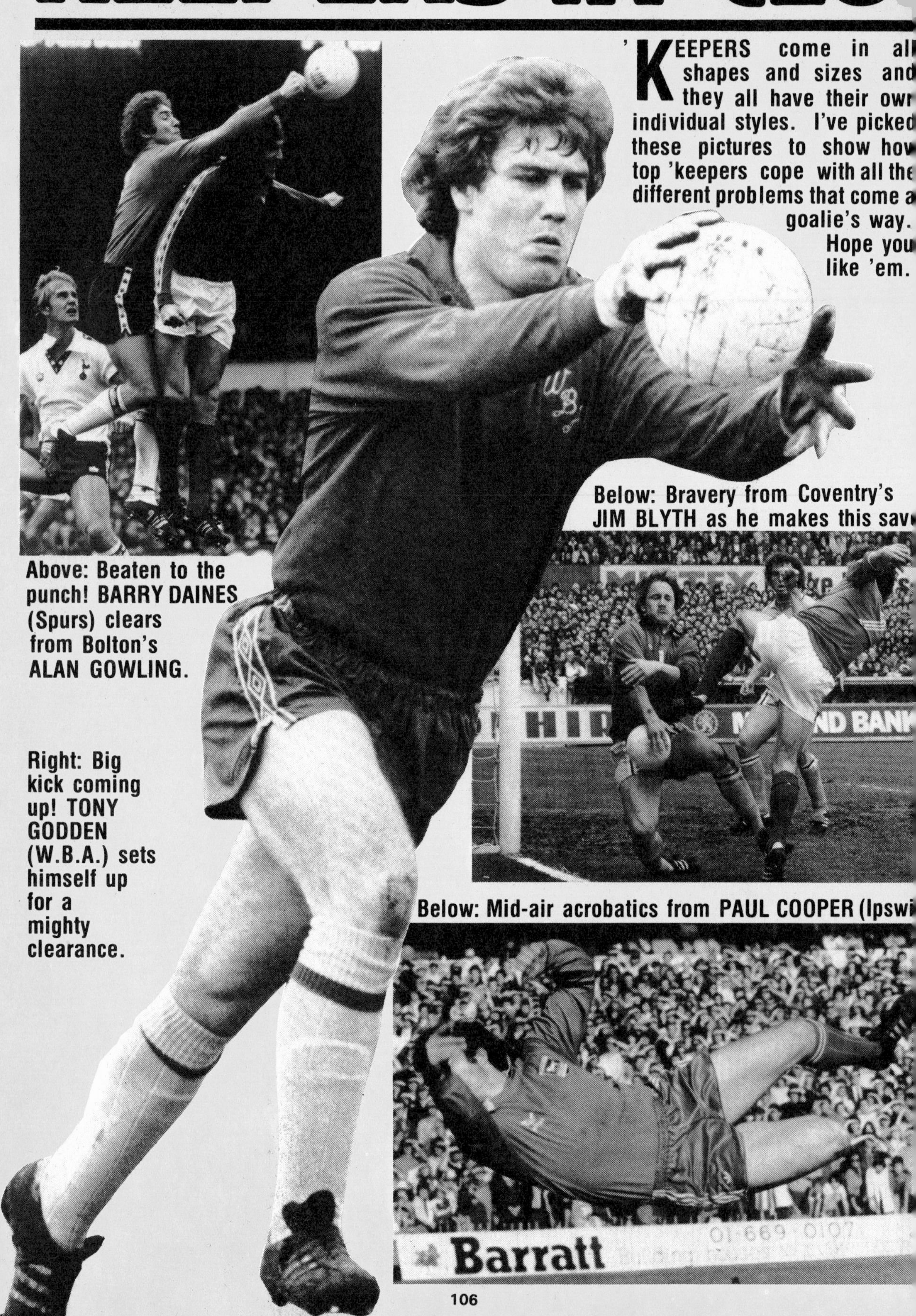

Above: Beaten to the punch! BARRY DAINES (Spurs) clears from Bolton's ALAN GOWLING.

Right: Big kick coming up! TONY GODDEN (W.B.A.) sets himself up for a mighty clearance.

Below: Bravery from Coventry's JIM BLYTH as he makes this sav

Below: Mid-air acrobatics from PAUL COOPER (Ipswi

Above: A desperate dive by Manchester United's GARY BAILEY.

Flying high is PAUL BRADSHAW (Wolves).

Above: Reaching high here is Manchester City's JOE CORRIGAN.

ow:
HN
RRIDGE
ystal Palace)
is CHRIS
NES of Spurs.

BOB-SLEIGH

Screaming down an ice-run at ninety miles per hour takes superb control and timing. And above all, ice-cool nerve.

To compete effectively at the top level of the sport requires tremendous technical know-how and a whole lot of financial backing.

Above all, it's financial backing that British teams have lacked in the past. Let's hope our bobsleighers get the assistance they deserve in 1981.

ICE SKATING

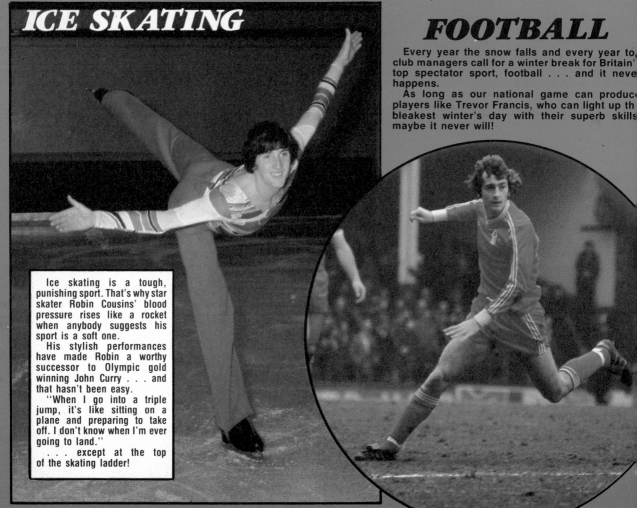

Ice skating is a tough, punishing sport. That's why star skater Robin Cousins' blood pressure rises like a rocket when anybody suggests his sport is a soft one.

His stylish performances have made Robin a worthy successor to Olympic gold winning John Curry . . . and that hasn't been easy.

"When I go into a triple jump, it's like sitting on a plane and preparing to take off. I don't know when I'm ever going to land."

. . . except at the top of the skating ladder!

FOOTBALL

Every year the snow falls and every year to, club managers call for a winter break for Britain' top spectator sport, football . . . and it neve happens.

As long as our national game can produc players like Trevor Francis, who can light up th bleakest winter's day with their superb skills maybe it never will!

WINTER

STAR FOCUS

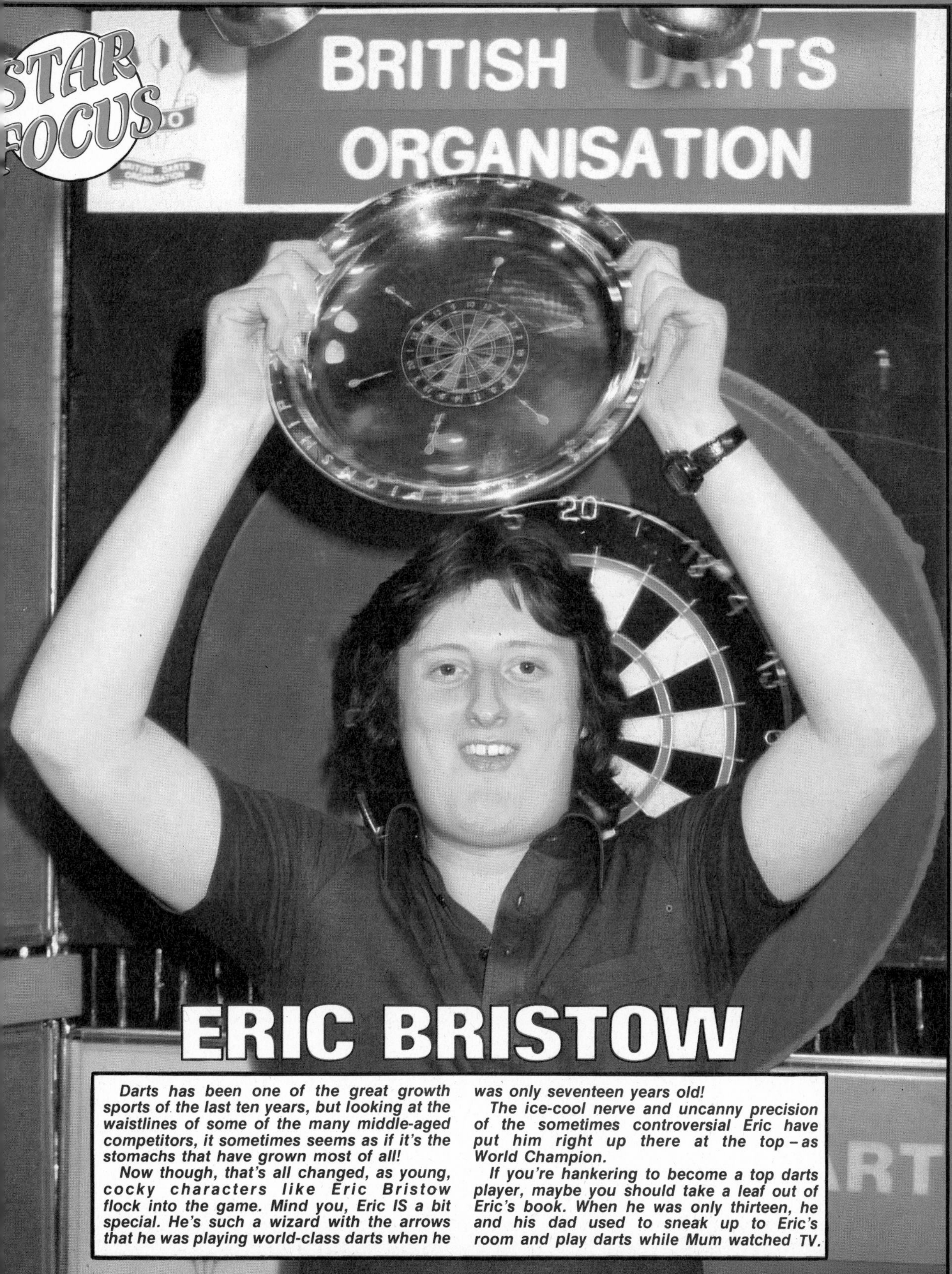

ERIC BRISTOW

Darts has been one of the great growth sports of the last ten years, but looking at the waistlines of some of the many middle-aged competitors, it sometimes seems as if it's the stomachs that have grown most of all!

Now though, that's all changed, as young, cocky characters like Eric Bristow flock into the game. Mind you, Eric IS a bit special. He's such a wizard with the arrows that he was playing world-class darts when he was only seventeen years old!

The ice-cool nerve and uncanny precision of the sometimes controversial Eric have put him right up there at the top – as World Champion.

If you're hankering to become a top darts player, maybe you should take a leaf out of Eric's book. When he was only thirteen, he and his dad used to sneak up to Eric's room and play darts while Mum watched TV.

POWERBOAT THRILLS ALL THE WAY WITH...
SPEED KINGS
After a series of spectacular wins in rallying, sports car racing and Formula 1 Grand Prix racing, Ron "Speedy" Hutton and his chief mechanic Greasy Tanner have been persuaded by small craft designer Paul Frazer to enter his revolutionary powerboat in the Paris Six Hour Powerboat Race . . .
WOW! Look at her go! You've designed a winner there, Paul!
Maybe, Ron, but now she's heading into rougher water. This'll show how she'll take to the conditions likely in the Paris Six Hour Race . . .
Just then . . .
A LOG . . . SHE'S GOING OVER . . .AAAHH! URGHHH!

Moments later . . .
Blimey! What a mess!
Take it easy, Alf, we'll soon get you to hospital!
That evening . . .
Bang goes Paris and my boat building business! Success would have brought orders flooding in, but now . . .
Hold on, Paul! There's still an experimental hull in your yard. If only we could get another engine — the one in the lake's a goner!
And so, next morning . . .
A situation like that could be remedied, gents! This looks like another job for Greasy Tanner's magic touch!
There it is! Luckily, Alf was over shallow water when he crashed. Now for the tricky bit . . .
We've got it, but are you sure you know what you're doing, Greasy?
Yeah — it's worth a try, Ron! Salt water would've ruined it, but this is a freshwater lake. Let's get it to the workshop!
Thanks for trying, but you'll never repair that engine in time! The race is in five days, and it'll take most of that to tow the boat to Paris!
I don't quit that easy! No engine has ever beaten me — AND THIS ONE WON'T BE THE FIRST!
If anyone can restore that engine, it's Greasy!
Then we'd better get this boat ready to receive it!
And later . . .
Try this for size, gents!
YOU'VE DONE IT! YOU'RE A BLOOMIN' MARVEL, GREASY!
I've replaced several parts which were damaged in the crash! She'll go like a bird now!
Then we're still in business! Come on — we've got a boat to finish!

And this is what Ron Hutton faces in the Paris Six Hour Race — an endurance test which has the habit of knocking the stuffing out of both driver and machine! You've got to have lightning-fast reflexes, knowledge of the water and bags of skill to cope with the high-flying speeds of powerboating — not to mention a whole lot of GUTS!

A day later the boat is ready for Ron's first practice session . . .
Blimey! I thought it would be like handling a car! The only similarity is the steering wheel!
WOW! The acceleration's really something! Greasy's done a great job on the engine!
WHOA! COME ROUND, YOU BRUTE!
Ron returns to the jetty . . .
Crikey, Ron! Looked like you were circuiting Brands Hatch there!
Practice! Practice! And soon Ron is taming the power-boat . . .
The boat is loaded up . . .
I'll finish off tuning the engine in Paris, Ron!
And I'll make some minor adjustments to the hull, there, too!
The overnight crossing brings their first rest for two days. Then, in Paris . . .
Make for the River Seine, Greasy! I want to see what I'm up against!
Ron joins the other drivers in the pre-race briefing . . .
We are now on the course, gentlemen — four kilometres of twisting river! The object is to complete as many circuits as you can in six hours!
Luckily for you, the river will be closed to all other traffic during the race!
Later . . .
Well, Ron, it's up to you! Without Alf as a co-pilot, you'll be on your own! It's going to be tough . . .
I can only do my best, boys!
FRAZER

And minutes later . . .
WE'RE OFF! I'm about to find out whether I'll ever make a powerboat driver!
OOOFF! What a battering!
The engine vibrations! The pounding! Paul's boat is taking it well – but can I?
Several laps later, Ron stops to refuel . . .
7
I'm getting the hang of it, Paul! I'll try to open her up a bit now!
They're throttling back for the bridge and the bend behind it – now's my chance to overtake them!
BLOOMIN' MANIAC! He'll never make it round the next bend at that speed!
DONE IT! I'M THROUGH!
SACRE BLEU! How can the British boat corner so tightly? The strain on the hull must be fantastic!
I'm picking up on time . . . HEY! THAT BOAT'S FLIPPING OVER!
Only one chance! I've got to hit that wave just right . . .

I'M BEING LIFTED OVER IT, BUT CAN THE HULL STAND THE IMPACT WHEN I LAND . . .?
URGHH!
Ron fights the pain and continues, but his troubles aren't over, as vibration takes its toll on one of the boats ahead . . .
The driver of No. 7 is injured, but he's still going . . .
Uhh . . . my arm feels like it's on fire!
MEIN GOTT! HIS ENGINE'S BREAKING LOOSE!
These two German boats are starting to swerve – something's wrong!
HIMMEL! HE'S OUT OF CONTROL AND FORCING ME WIDE!
As both boats come to a disastrous end, Ron senses big trouble . . .
AAARGHH!
Blimey! It's like a minefield! At this speed, hitting any of the debris will crack open my hull like an eggshell!
Holy cow! Did ya see that?
Yeah — that Limey craft could turn on a dime! Went through that wreckage as if it wasn't there!
At the final refuelling . . .
That's it, Ron — time to quit! Apart from that arm injury, you're done in!
QUIT? When I'm in third position? Don't talk daft! Besides — it only hurts when I laugh!

Ron roars into action!
That's me past Rene Le Bois, which leaves only current champion Bob Skeldon – AND ME!
Look at Ron go, Paul! He'll soon be past the American!
Don't be too sure, Greasy! They're equal on laps, and Skeldon's an old hand at the powerboat game!
This is my last chance to find out whether the Paul Frazer hull is special, or not!
I'VE DONE IT – THROUGH ON THE INSIDE!
BLIMEY! WE'RE FIRST! YOUR BOAT'S A WINNER, MATE!
NO MORE THAN RON IS, GREASY! WHAT A RACE!
Once the ceremonies are over . . .
There's enormous interest in the design of the Frazer hull, not to mention the unusual feat of one man racing, and winning, single-handed . . .
Mister Hutton is unavailable for comment! Try asking him in twelve hours! You see — HE'S HAD A BUSY DAY!
Z-Z-Z-Z-Z-Z
The End

STAR ★ FOCUS

Goals are his game, ANDY GRAY is his name!

When Andy Gray signed for Wolverhampton Wanderers back in 1979 he set a record transfer fee of £1,500,000. Many people thought that the Scottish striker would have signed for a more fashionable and successful club, say Liverpool or Arsenal. However, Andy, as sharp off the field as he is on it, knew what he was doing. He thought very carefully about the whole situation and finally put pen to paper in front of 40,000 fans at Molineux.

The fearless goalscorer was intent on putting the snarl back into the Wolves, a snarl that had been sadly missing for almost two decades.

He and the quicksilver John Richards immediately built up an understanding and now they are one of the best striking duos in the Football League.

Andy has shown everyone that he made no mistake in signing for Wolverhampton, the goals have come regularly for him, and their success can be attributed to his signing.

Many players might have cracked under the strain of being worth 1½ million pounds but Andy didn't. He responded the only way he knows — by sticking the ball in the net!

IT'S A FUNNY GAME!

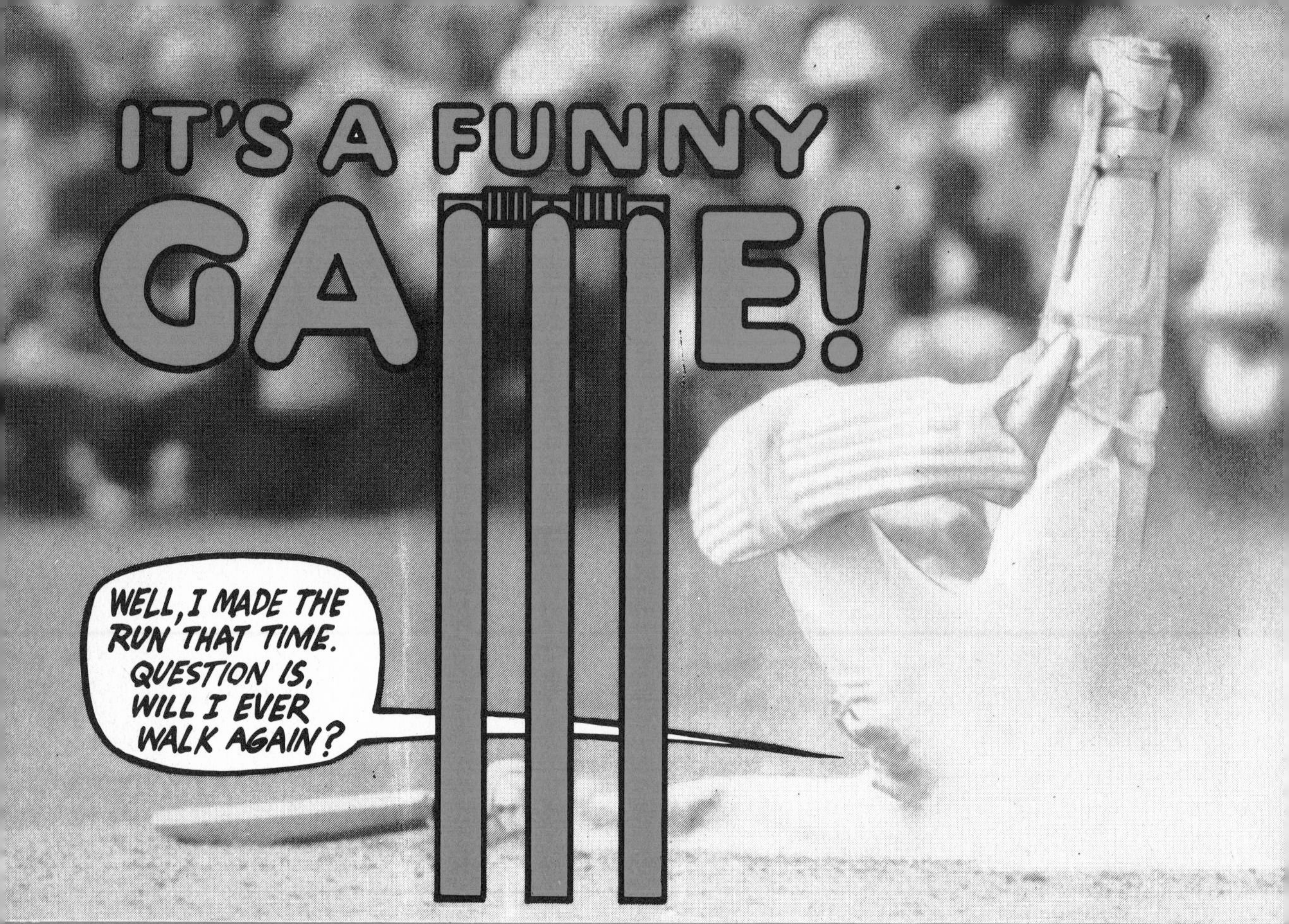

WELL, I MADE THE RUN THAT TIME. QUESTION IS, WILL I EVER WALK AGAIN?

Big crowds, sparkling fielding, dynamic bowling and spectacular batting, they're all part of the cricket scene.

But there is another side to England's great national game. Even in the red-hot atmosphere of Test and County cricket, there's always time for a laugh . . .

THE BALL WASN'T UP TO MUCH–BUT IT'S GOT TO BE 9·8 FOR ARTISTIC MERIT!

...NINE...TEN...OUT!

YOU'RE RIGHT, WITH TWO BATS I'LL MAYBE STAND SOME CHANCE AGAINST THIS BOWLING!

WISH I HADN'T JUST REMEMBERED THAT OLD SAYING– WHAT GOES UP...

SOMETIMES I WONDER HOW I STAND THE PACE AND ACTION OF TOP CLASS CRICKET.

SPORTS Crossword

MR AOKI WILL USE 10 ACROSS.

ACROSS

1. SCOTTISH SECOND DIVISION TEAM. (11)
7. THIS MIGHT DEVELOP BETWEEN TWO OPPOSING PLAYERS. (6)
8. ROSCOE TANNER'S GAME. (6)
9. SHE MAY RUN AT 5 DOWN. (4)
10. A GOLFING ITEM. (3)
11. USED IN A TUG O' WAR. (4)
12. EXPERIENCED MIDFIELDER DOES THIS TO THE PLAY. (5)
15. HAS— _____ SOMETIMES COME BACK. (5)
19. YOU MIGHT GET THIS IF YOU TACKLE APPREHENSIVELY. (4)
20. A HOLE-IN-ONE. (3)
21. . . . SET AND MATCH. (4)
22. REFEREE'S DECISIONS ARE OFTEN THIS. (6)
23. HE'S NOW CALLED A STRIKER. (6)
25. NO PLAYER WANTS THESE. (11)

★

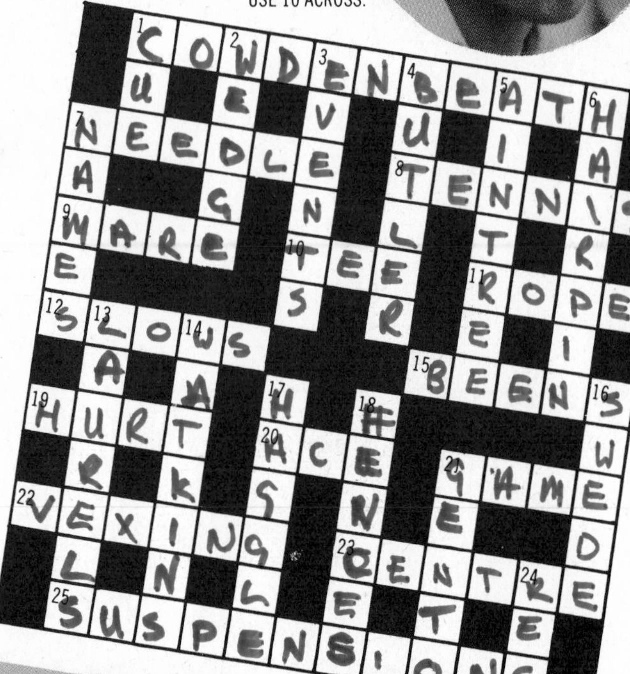

DOWN

1. TERRY GRIFFITHS USES ONE. (3)
2. IT'S SOMETIMES CALLED A 10-IRON. (5)
3. THERE'S TEN OF THESE IN THE DECATHLON. (6)
4. THIS PETER WILL USE 2 DOWN (6)
5. RED RUM'S HOME COURSE? (7)
6. DANGEROUS TYPE OF BEND. (7)
7. THE LINE-UP'S FULL OF THEM. (5)
13. HONOURS FOR MOTOR RACING CHAMPIONS? (7)
14. THIS SPEEDY GLEN IS IN THE U.S.A. (7)
16. BORG IS ONE. (5)
17. MANAGERS MIGHT DO THIS OVER THE PRICE OF A PLAYER. (6)
18. FOUND IN A STEEPLECHASE. (6)
21. BRILLIANT EX-REAL MADRID AND SPAIN LEFT WINGER. (5)
24. A SHORT RESERVE. (3)

THE WORLD FAMOUS RED RUM. SEE 5 DOWN.

No. 9, BUT WHAT DID HE USED TO BE CALLED? SEE 23 ACROSS.

ANSWERS. **Across** 1. COWDENBEATH. 7. NEEDLE. 8. TENNIS. 9. MARE. 10. TEE. 11. ROPE. 12. SLOWS 15. BEENS. 19. HURT. 20. ACE. 21. GAME. 22. VEXING. 23. CENTRE. 25. SUSPENSIONS. **Down** 1. CUE. 2. WEDGE. 3. EVENTS. 4. BUTLER. 5. AINTREE. 6. HAIRPIN. 7. NAMES. 13. LAURELS. 14. WATKINS. 16. SWEDE. 17. HAGGLE. 18. FENCES. 21. GENTO. 24. RES.

Windsurf... or Bust!
HI — my name's Norman and, like all the other lads in the Scoop office, I like to try my hand at most sports. Usually, this means a game of badminton or table tennis, but a few months ago, when the Scoop Editor asked me if I'd mind getting wet in the middle of winter, I reckoned they had something rather different in mind for me — HOW RIGHT I WAS! A reader had written in and challenged one of the Scoop staff to take up WIND-SURFING! Guess which mug volunteered to take the course?
Windsurfing expert Alasdair Govan was my tutor...
Well, Norman, before you get near any water, there's a lot to learn about windsurfing. There's the theory of sailing, the all-important safety aspect, and, you've got to know all about your sailboard.
Once the boom is rigged to the mast and sail, I'll fix it to the sailboard simulator I keep for dry-land tuition.
Okay, Alasdair. I'm with you so far!
On the board simulator, we can get the same conditions that you'll experience on water. You'll see that the bottom of the mast is fitted with a universal joint which fits into the board.
For the next two hours, Alasdair explained the ins and outs of windsurfing. The way he did it made it look easy – or so I thought!
Note the position of my feet and hands. This is known as sailing position.

Then it was my turn!
Got to keep my weight centred on the board, and the wind to my back . . .
Knees bent, a steady pull on the uphall line and up comes the mast. So far, so good . . .
That's it — get your feet into position, take hold with the mast hand and bring the mast up to vertical. Now let go with your left hand and slide it along the boom . . .
And bingo! Sailing position!
Hey – this isn't too difficult!
For the next hour I practised the technical side of windsurfing, and with the proper stance, I could feel the wind filling the sail . . .
Okay, that's three hours tuition all told. It's about time we had you down to the water!
Oh, blimey! It'll be freezing!
But first the safety precautions.
Phew! This is more like it! A nice, safe dinghy to fish me out!
Hup! Handy trailer this! It'll do fine to carry me off to hospital once I drown!
And then . . .
I'm more used to putting on football strips than wet suits, but if it helps to keep me warm . . .

Ten minutes later . . .
We're off!
Well, it looks calm enough, but . . .

Just remember everything I've taught you, Norman. Now rig the sail like I showed you, and I'll fix you up with a life jacket. Then, it's all up to you —

Paddling out from the shore, I was soon ready for my first attempt at windsurfing!
Knees bent, wind directly behind me . . . hope I remember everything!

A steady pull on the uphall line . . .

Nearly there – got to let the water out of the sail as Alasdair told me –

That's the mast vertical and the wind's filling the sail. Now if I 'sheet in' by pulling the boom back towards me with the right hand, I should move forward . . . hopefully!

Easy? That's a laugh!
Brr! Reckon I did something wrong!
But I got my balance wrong, and . . .
HEY! AAAAHH!
Well, that was a disastrous start! I can only improve . . .
And . . .
Got it going, Alasdair! WHEEE!
Get that mast vertical or you'll be swimming again!
That's it – perfect!
After another hour of mixed fortune, Alasdair took my tuition a step further . . .
Okay, now we'll try tacking — that means a complete change in the direction you're sailing by moving your position on the board.

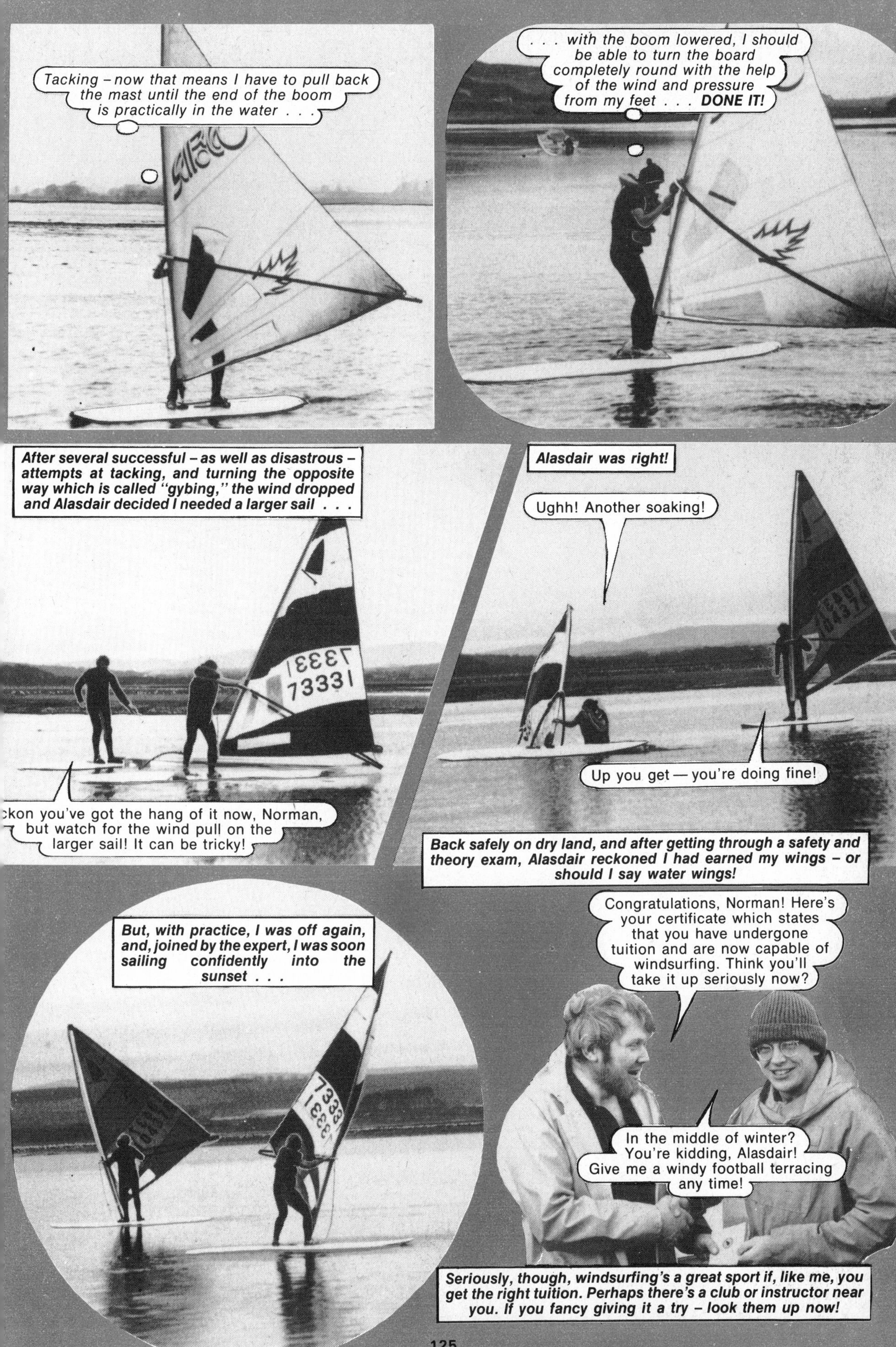
Tacking – now that means I have to pull back the mast until the end of the boom is practically in the water . . .
. . . with the boom lowered, I should be able to turn the board completely round with the help of the wind and pressure from my feet . . . DONE IT!
After several successful – as well as disastrous – attempts at tacking, and turning the opposite way which is called "gybing," the wind dropped and Alasdair decided I needed a larger sail . . .
7333I
73331
kon you've got the hang of it now, Norman, but watch for the wind pull on the larger sail! It can be tricky!
Alasdair was right!
Ughh! Another soaking!
Up you get — you're doing fine!
Back safely on dry land, and after getting through a safety and theory exam, Alasdair reckoned I had earned my wings – or should I say water wings!
But, with practice, I was off again, and, joined by the expert, I was soon sailing confidently into the sunset . . .
Congratulations, Norman! Here's your certificate which states that you have undergone tuition and are now capable of windsurfing. Think you'll take it up seriously now?
In the middle of winter? You're kidding, Alasdair! Give me a windy football terracing any time!
Seriously, though, windsurfing's a great sport if, like me, you get the right tuition. Perhaps there's a club or instructor near you. If you fancy giving it a try – look them up now!

YAMAHA
KENNY
YAMAHA